— Praise for *The Trouble with Paris* —

Mark has something fresh to say about what can kill your soul and who can salvage it.

—JOHN ORTBERG, Pastor of Menlo Park Presbyterian Church
and author of *When the Game is Over, It All Goes Back in the Box*

These are great tools for everyone trying to find the Way, the Truth, and the Life in a world of shortcuts, deception, and death. Amid the noise and seductions of our culture, may Mark's work help us to be both relevant and peculiar to this chaotic world. May we raise up a generation of radical non-conformists with everything that is wrong in the world, a generation that turns the world upside down so that it aligns with the Kingdom of God.

—SHANE CLAIBORNE, Author of *The Irresistible
Revolution: Living as an Ordinary Radical*
www.thesimpleway.org

Mark Sayers is something of a spiritual genius who is able to both name and diagnose the angst of an entire generation caught up in the web of consumerism and hyperreality. This book is laced with the kind of wise and prophetic insights that take the reader to the heart of some of the most important issues of our age. Nothing less than a clue to the spiritual healing of a generation lies hidden in the pages of this book.

—ALAN HIRSCH, Author of *The Forgotten Ways* and author
(with Michael Frost) of *The Shaping of Things to Come*.
Alan is founding director of *Forge Mission Training Network*.

Mark Sayers' new book *The Trouble with Paris* is outstanding. Well informed, insightful, articulate, and down to earth are just a few thoughts that come to mind when describing this *tour de force*. Sayers has a unique ability to put his finger on the pulse of contemporary culture and Christianity, and he proves to be a capable guide through the thickets of that which is counterfeit and fake. Today we're submersed in the media driven and publicity shaped hollow promises of hyperreality, which are driving us to embrace the unreal and consequently an impoverished spirituality. Reading this powerful book will help us get back to the real and lead us to a rediscovery of our spiritual bearings for the present and the future.

In working with Swiss L'Abri for over twenty years now, my take on this book is that it's exactly what we need to get our priorities aligned with living in God's reality, instead of trying and failing to make it up as we go along. Hyperreality is deceptively addictive, and if we are to touch a generation of people for the sake of Christ, it is books like Sayers' *The Trouble with Paris* that will help pave the way. Highly recommended.

—DR. GREGORY J. LAUGHERY, Author of
Living Spirituality: Illuminating the Path and
teacher with L'Abri Fellowship, Switzerland

The Trouble with *Paris*

Following Jesus in a World of Plastic Promises

Mark Sayers

THOMAS NELSON
Since 1798

NASHVILLE   DALLAS   MEXICO CITY   RIO DE JANEIRO   BEIJING

I would like to dedicate this book to my family,

who do so much to remind me of God's reality:

My wife, Trudi;

my parents, Garry & Joy;

my brother, Glen;

my sister, Melody;

my sister-in-law, Theary;

and, of course, my daughter,

little Grace,

who was born during the final editing of this book.

© 2008 by Mark Sayers

Published in Nashville, Tennessee, by Thomas Nelson. Thomas Nelson is a registered trademark of Thomas Nelson, Inc.

Thomas Nelson, Inc. titles may be purchased in bulk for educational, business, fund-raising, or sales promotional use. For information, please e-mail SpecialMarkets@ThomasNelson.com.

Scripture quotations are taken from the HOLY BIBLE: NEW INTERNATIONAL VERSION®. © 1973, 1978, 1984 by International Bible Society. Used by permission of Zondervan Publishing House. All rights reserved.

Library of Congress Cataloging-in-Publication Data available upon request.

ISBN 978-0-8499-1999-2

Printed in the United States of America

08 09 10 11 12 RRD 9 8 7 6 5 4 3 2 1

Contents

Contents

Part 3 God's Reality

Acknowledgments

I would like to thank those who helped this book come to life. Thanks to my wife, Trudi, for all of her love and support. Thanks to my parents, Garry and Joy Sayers, and my fellow director at Uber ministries, Sarah Deutscher, for reading through the initial drafts and offering such great feedback. Thanks to Matt Baugher, Jenn McNeil, and the wonderful team at Thomas Nelson. Thanks to the fantastic leadership team at the Red Network—Martin de Graaf, John Jensen, and Cath Mckinney—for their prayers and support during this process.

Thanks to Ben Catford, A. J. Clifford, and the team at Room 3 for believing so much in the talk, which became a DVD, which became a book. Thanks to Alan and Deborah Hirsch, whose influence on my life can be found throughout the pages of this book. Thanks to the Forge tribe for providing so many platforms to get this message out. Thanks to all the stimulating people at the Red Network, especially my congregation and community at Red East, who show me so many touches of the coming kingdom. Thanks to Nick Wight, whose help in this process was invaluable. Thanks to Brett Rice for his assistance. Thanks to Dave Ridgeway, whose generosity helped in many practical ways. Thanks to Nicholas Wightman, whose

Acknowledgments

regular conversations with me about faith, life, and culture sparked the initial idea for this message. Thanks also to the Brikwerk Art Collective, whose creative influence on my thinking can be seen flowing through this book. And lastly, thanks to the cities of Whitehorse and Box Hill for providing so much inspiration during the writing of this book.

Part 1

Hyperreality

ONE

Why Your Faith
Does Not Work

She looked like a girl who had it all. She was strikingly beautiful, confident, and hip. Half the guys in the room were looking at her, and all the girls in the room wanted to be her. She had ticked all the boxes: she was deeply involved in her church, had a high-paying job, traveled all over the world, and had a social life most of us would be jealous of, with a bevy of male suitors. Yet for her this meant nothing.

She looked me square in the eye with pain in her face and told me, "I was promised an awesome life!" I was immediately thrown. This girl had everything that society tells us will make us happy. Yet as I listened to the reality of her life, I realized that nothing could be further from the truth. Behind the glamorous exterior was a person who was struggling, who was unsure of who she was, who struggled with depression and with the dissatisfaction of constantly feeling as if she needed more. Her life was in limbo, and she was constantly waiting for this awesome life to turn up, yet it never came. She had finally come to the realization that she was miserable, and she felt very, very ripped off.

This is a story that can be heard among those who have left the Christian faith because it didn't deliver them the perfect life they believed they were promised. It can also be heard in the dissatisfaction and frustrations of those who still have faith. And finally, it can be heard in those who never had faith yet invested all of their hope in the fact that one day the perfect future will arrive. If we are to live lives of meaning, satisfaction, and happiness, it is essential that we understand what effects our culture has on our quality of life and quality of faith. Let's begin with faith.

SOMETHING IS EATING YOUR FAITH

Throughout the developed Western world, a corrosive epidemic is eating away at the faith lives of Christians. It assails us in our darkest moments; it comes to us at three o'clock in the morning when we can't sleep. It confronts us at every corner, three to ten thousand times a day. It whispers to our hearts that we've got it wrong, that our faith should not be in Jesus Christ of Nazareth but in something else. In this context your faith is getting torn apart and most likely will not survive. Contrary to popular belief, you and your friends probably won't lose your faith because of sex, drugs, or doubt but for a much more insidious reason. Sure, you can fight it; you can think, *It won't be me*. But how do you fight an enemy you can't name, an opponent you can't see?

The thing that will eat away at your faith, make it impotent, and finally kill it off cannot easily be named. It is a framework, a formation system, an entire worldview. It tells us how to live and how to act. It speaks to our sense of identity. It shapes our personality. It tells us what to love, what to commit to, and what to have hope in. It is a virus that eats our faith from the inside out. This virus is the allure of the hyperreal world.

If you want to blame someone or something for your life not ending up as wonderfully as you were led to believe it would, a good place to start is the cultural phenomenon called hyperreality. The combination of a hyperconsumer culture, mass media, and rampant individualism has created a world of hyperreality. What is hyperreality? It's a term I learned from a French guy named Jean Baudrillard. He was a twentieth-century philosopher who took a trip across America, visiting places like Las Vegas and Disneyland. He said that our culture had become hyperreal, meaning that we could now have things that were even better than the real thing. The media-drenched world in which we live has overextended our expectations of life.

Following are some examples of hyperreality:

+ A fairly pretty girl works as a model to support her studies. She does a photo shoot for a fashion magazine. The photographer skillfully uses wardrobe, lighting, and make-up during the shoot. After the shoot, computers are used to take away the model's imperfections and to improve her overall look. The magazine hits the newsstands, and through the magic of technology, a fairly pretty girl has been turned into a stunningly beautiful cover model. Thousands of women buy the magazine and wonder why they cannot be as beautiful and glamorous as the model on the cover, not realizing that if they walked past the actual model in the street, they would not even notice her.

✦ A man drives to work every day past a billboard advertising vacations on an idyllic Pacific island. As he works in his stressful office job, he fantasizes about relaxing on the white beaches under the palm trees of the beautiful Pacific paradise he sees on the billboard. The man purchases a two-week vacation on the island. Upon arrival, the man discovers that for most of the year it rains. He tries swimming only to find that the coral cuts up his feet and that he has to be careful not to contract malaria from the mosquitoes on the island. The man spends most of his vacation watching satellite TV in his resort room.

✦ A group of friends share a house. Each week they watch a situation comedy about a group of friends who share a house as well. As they watch, each person wonders to why they cannot be as close and as happy as the characters in the sitcom. In real life, the cast of actors cannot stand each other.

Hyperreality means that often we cannot tell the difference between what advertising tells us about products, places, and people and what they are like in the real world. In the rush to sell us things, corporations have sacrificed reality; truth telling is gone. Sociologist Krishan Kumar explains:

> Our world has become so saturated with images and symbols that a new "electronic reality" has been created, whose effect is to obliterate any sense of an objective reality lying behind the images and symbols. In this "simulated" world, images become objects, rather than reflecting them; reality becomes hyper-reality. In hyper-reality it is no longer possible to distinguish the imaginary from the real . . . the true from the false.[1]

An ad by the New York tourism board is not going to tell us about the street crime, high prices, pollution, and poverty we would find in the city. Rather, they are going to show us the New York we know from countless movies and TV shows such as *Seinfeld*, *Sex and the City*, and *Friends*. And if they are smart, they will use the Frank Sinatra song, "New York, New York" to top it all off. After seeing an advertisement for New York and experiencing New York, we would be left scratching our heads and asking, "Which is the real New York—the metropolis we know from our years of watching popular culture or the actual city situated on the East Coast?" We would have confused the symbol (the popular culture's imagined New York) with the real city. Of course, the popular Hollywood version of New York would be the more attractive one. This is hyperreality. It gives us a world of symbols that are detached from the reality of what they are supposed to be symbolizing, and they appear more attractive than the original objects they are representing.

TWO

Welcome to
Hyperreality

HYPERREALITY AND THE DEATH OF REALITY

I am standing in a supermarket aisle, looking at the gossip magazines that are strategically placed at the point of purchase. One magazine has an image on its cover of two famous A-list Hollywood actors who have been in a much-publicized relationship. The shot is blurry and obviously has been captured by the paparazzi. The image shows the couple running to a waiting car with their hands up, hiding their faces from the glare of the camera. The magazine's headline sensationally declares that the image is evidence the relationship is on the rocks and divorce is inevitable. However, on the cover of the gossip magazine's main competitor is the same paparazzi shot of the famous lovers, except that this time the headline informs me that the couple have never been happier and are planning for a baby. Which magazine do I believe? Is either even close to the truth of what is happening in the love life of the famous couple?

I turn on the news and see that a car bomb has exploded in the Middle East. The left-wing cable news network reports the bombing as a blow to the U.S. government's foreign policy.

I turn to another cable network—this one with a right-wing bias—and the station is reporting on the same terrorist attack, using the same images, but the anchor is speaking of the bombing as a justification of the government's foreign policy. Who do I believe? Reality has become very blurred. The messages we receive through the media throughout our daily lives are not "value free"; they are filled with ideologies and spin.

The sheer volume of competing messages threatens to overwhelm us. The age of technological boom in which we live offers us almost constant exposure to the media; it is almost impossible to escape. At my local mall, I cannot use the restroom without being exposed to pop culture. Pop songs are piped into the stalls, advertisements are placed above the urinal, and the hand dryer plays video ads as I dry my hands. This constant exposure to media has deeply changed how we view reality. In the face of so much exposure to media's version of life, we must ask whether we are more influenced by the model of reality we find in our everyday lives or by the model we are shown by media. The world we see in the media will always seem attractive and alluring, because almost all of the media to which we are exposed is produced with the agenda of getting us to buy something, be it a product, experience, opinion, or service.

BETTER LIVING THROUGH HYPERREALITY

It is in the interest of those who saturate our world with media to paint an image of a world that is infinitely more appealing than the reality of our lives. But the catch is that the more we are exposed to the hyperreal messages of media, the more dissatisfied we become with our own lives. The hyperreal world shows us people whose lives are like ours but better—the woman who uses the same shampoo as we do but is more attractive; the family who has the same amount of kids as we have but looks happier and more satisfied; the guy who uses the same deodorant as we do but manages to pick up girls who look like supermodels. How can our everyday realities compete with the promises of the hyperreal world? How can my life of getting up, going to work, shopping at the supermarket, and cleaning my toilet compete with the sexy, slick version of life that is presented to me by hyperreality?

The clear message behind hyperreality is that if we are to have lives of worth, happiness, and well-being, we need to move our lives into the hyperreal world. We need to imitate the lives we see in movies, in advertising, in lifestyle magazines, in music videos, and on television—then we will be happy.

The problem is that the lifestyles we see on TV are not real; they are simulations, illusions. Therefore, as theologian Vincent

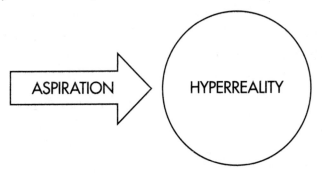

Miller observes, "Along with sporting events, rock concerts, shopping malls, and magazines, television provides images of the good life that bring virtual vicarious fulfillment. In the face of a spectacular world with which our everyday lives could never compete, we are reduced to passive spectators, consumers of illusions."[1] Instead of our lives being filled with the excitement and energy we observe in the hyperreal world, we actually find ourselves becoming consumers of someone else's life. We sit zombielike, watching images of what life "should be like" as we read catalogs, watch the lives of celebrities on television, and lust after the latest consumer item we are told we "must" own. We end up trading our reality for a simulation of reality in which happiness and fulfillment are always just out of reach. We become detached from our actual lives, reaching always for simulations, mirages of real life that can never be reached. We become slaves to the romance of "I will be happy when . . ."

THE ROMANCE OF "I WILL BE HAPPY WHEN . . . "

It is a perfect spring evening. I am sitting in a trendy restaurant in an even trendier plaza. Outside, the downtown skyline sparkles; inside, the young, hip, beautiful, and fashionable sparkle as well. The interior decorations complement the stylish French house music that is being played, which complements the stylish modern cuisine. But as I look around, all is not well in paradise. I am alerted to this fact by the couple on my left, who are not impressed with our fabulous dining experience. "How amazing would it be to be in New York right now?" is quickly followed by "We should have gone to that stunning little Tibetan restaurant." All across the restaurant, furtive glances are being exchanged as couples on dates are looking for someone better, girls are looking at what other girls are wearing, boys are looking at what other boys are wearing, and whole tables are looking to see if other tables are having more fun than they are. It all makes for a pretty paranoid room; the one thing that's sure is that no one really seems to be enjoying the view. Happiness is always what someone else is doing; it is always somewhere else. This is a culture that has embraced the romance of "I will be happy when . . ."

My friend Martin was for many years a relationship counselor. He told me that often when a couple begins experiencing difficulties in their relationship, they plan to go on a vacation or move to a new house. They begin to apply layers of romantic idealism about this new place to which they will move, never realizing that the problems they are dealing with are inside them. This is true not just of couples but of all consumers in the hyperreality culture. Thus, in the hyperreality world, happiness is always just around the corner, yet always out of reach.

This sense of incompleteness powers the global economy. Happiness is always postponed; fulfillment and meaning can never be found. In many ways, it is like trying to reach the horizon; you can always see it and you can walk toward it, but it stays away at the same distance. Hyperreality is an "I will be happy when . . ." existence. The space following the "when" will be different for everyone and will constantly change. But the principle of postponing happiness is the same for everyone who operates in the hyperreal world. So no matter how affluent or comfortable our lives become, we will always be looking over our shoulder at something better. In many ways this "I will be happy when . . ." culture becomes the ultimate "addiction" culture as people enter the addictive downward spiral, always needing a bigger hit to satisfy their growing cravings and becoming less free in the process.

Hyperreality helps us understand why so many of us struggle to reconcile the lives we lead with the lives we *expect* to lead. Understanding hyperreality also sheds light on the reason so many of us struggle to make our faith relevant to our daily lives. If we are to move forward, we must examine the role that consumerism plays in creating our hyperreal condition. For it is our culture of hyperconsumerism that creates so much of the dissatisfaction we feel about our actual lives.

THREE

The Whole of Life
As Shopping: Hyperconsumerism

I am watching a hip-hop video. In the video a world-famous rapper is lyrically taunting his rivals. The camera focuses in on his diamond-studded "bling" necklace. He is pictured surrounded by several tricked-out sports cars. On his feet are special-edition personalized sneakers. The retro football jersey he is wearing can only be bought in one specialized store and is hunted down by "cool hunters" who spend months searching for rare sportswear in secondhand stores. As he is rapping, he holds up a latest model cell phone, and unbeknownst to the rapper's fans, the cell phone's appearance in the video is no accident but the result of a carefully executed underground campaign by a top New York public relations firm. Surrounding the hip-hop star are several models who, although diverse in their ethnicity, are united in their highly sexualized dance moves and lack of clothing.

The message is clear: the fact that the rapper can afford all of these products is evidence that he is at the top of his game as a successful businessman. Even the girls function as consumer items. The message is that he is so rich he can afford multiple attractive sex partners. The music video (which is really just a three-minute advertisement) ends, and we cross back to the set of the cable music video show, owned by a giant global corporation. The VJ who is hosting the show is wearing clothes that are made by a subsidiary of the same global corporation.

The VJ then welcomes to the show a popular Hollywood starlet to talk about her new blockbuster film (which is produced by the same corporation that owns the music video channel). In the movie, the starlet drives around in a cute little convertible that is placed in the film by a motor company that is also owned by the same global corporation. After the brief interview, the starlet is allowed to pick her favorite music video. She chooses one by a young punk band that just happens to be on a label owned by the giant global corporation that pays the starlet's wages. The video features the punk band singing about their teenage sense of rage and alienation. It does not have the flamboyant luxury items of the hip-hop video; however, the lead singer's shoes and the drummer's cap reveal that a skateboarding shoe company sponsors the band. This company just so happens to be owned by a larger worldwide sportswear company of which a major shareholder is our friendly giant global corporation, which owns everything we have just spoken about. Welcome to the world of hyperconsumerism—a world where the whole of life has become a shopping experience.

Advertising assaults us almost every waking moment of the day. You sit down to eat your breakfast and find advertising on the cereal. The music you listen to on your car radio on the way to work is constantly interrupted with on-air ads. As you drive through a contemporary Western city, almost every spare space is covered with advertising. Some advertising agencies have even flirted with the idea of projecting an advertisement onto the moon!

Increasingly subtler ways are being used to sell products. Consumers often don't even know they are experiencing advertising. For example, imagine you are sitting at a bar on a Saturday night, and an attractive stranger strikes a flirtatious conversation with you. In the midst of your conversation, this person buys you a new type of drink, recommending its attributes. After a good chat the stranger disappears into the night. You have just been duped. The stranger had little or no interest in you apart from being paid by the drink company to engage in this covert style of advertising. The companies interested in the youth market will find and pay the coolest kids in school to wear and recommend their products. Thirty-year-old men, working for advertisers, will log on to teenage chat rooms, masquerading as teenagers to surreptitiously extol various products. Companies now pay huge fees to have their products featured in and used by characters in both film and television.

Advertisers will continue seeking more and more effective means of making us want to buy their products. Part of the reason we find ourselves in such a position as a culture is that advertising has taken a very different approach in our lifetimes.

FUNCTION AS MEANING

Once upon a time products were sold on the merit of their function. People were told, "Buy this bar of soap because it will get you clean"; "Buy this suit because it is well made"; "Buy this car because it is safe and will be economical for your family." This practice lasted for only a short time as advertisers found that the more they advertised to people, the more consumers developed a kind of antibody to advertising. People began to distrust what advertisers had to say when every product claimed to be the most functional. Even so, the advertising industry was prepared to rise to this challenge. Thus the history of advertising is the story of the development of more and more ingenious ways to convince people to buy products that they need. Moreover, advertisers have made trillions of dollars convincing people to buy products they do not need.

This method of advertising has become ubiquitous. If we are to believe the thousands of messages to which we are exposed on a daily basis, products have almost special powers. Buying the right kind of screwdriver set will make models want to sleep with you; buying the right talcum powder will make you a more caring mother; buying the right kind of handbag will make your coworkers and neighbors jealous of you; an SUV can make you feel more powerful; a cell phone can help you connect with your kids better. More and more, advertising has little to do with the actual product being sold. Rather, we are sold products on the basis of symbolic meanings. We are so used to this kind of selling that we do not blink an eye at the outlandish promises we are presented with each day. The sad reality is that for the most part, we actually believe the promises.

Sex isn't the only gimmick advertisers use. They also gain great results from making us feel inadequate or incomplete. If we are made to feel that unless we buy a particular product, we are "not cool" or "not a good mother" or are "out of touch," we are more likely to buy it. In fact, advertising even takes aim at our anxiety over our social position, challenging us to move ourselves up the social ladder by buying the right products.

Even our need for connection and community in an increasingly disconnected society is exploited by the consumer culture. Many today relate to each other not by ethnicity, family background, religion, or geography, but by a common loyalty to a product. For many youth, their potential to belong to a particular group is determined by making the right consumer choices. We find that products have become the way we relate to each other and find people "just like us," as cultural critic Daniel Harris explains: "In a fragmented society in which major institutions like the church and the community no longer play the same role of bringing people together, owning identical possessions becomes one of the chief ways in which we experience community, overcoming our isolation through shared patterns of consumption."[1]

Harris is right in linking the rise of this meaning-laden form of advertising to the decline of civic institutions and religion in the West. Advertisers understand that in a culture where religion is relegated to the private sphere, people live in a secular vacuum where they are deeply susceptible to messages that speak to our innermost needs. One of the legacies of the West's Christian heritage is that for hundreds of years humans were seen as bearers of the image of God. The story of Genesis taught us that everyone, no matter how rich or how poor, fit or frail, talented or feeble, was created in God's image. Today, however, this ethic is nowhere to be seen. Our need for identity is no longer found in our divine creation. Instead, we are told that we are to find our identity in the things that we consume. The unspoken message we receive every day is that our worth and identity can be judged by what we buy.

When we move from a culture that uses consumerism as a tool—that is, the buying and selling of products that we need on the basis of their function—to a culture where the framework of consumerism affects almost every aspect of life, the whole of life becomes like going to the mall. This is a world where we are effectively discipled by hyperconsumerism. We are told what is important, what to value, what to put our effort into, what to find meaning in. Theologian John F. Kavanaugh points out that hyperconsumerism works as a complete system that controls our reality. "With consumerism functioning as a system of reality . . . it does not just affect the way we shop. It affects the way we think and feel, the way we love and pray, the way we evaluate our enemies, the way we relate to our spouses and children."[2]

We are thus formed by hyperconsumer culture, and the irony is that ultimately our whole lives become products; we become commodities ourselves. Instead of using things, things now use us. We are facing a future where more and more things in life that once were free are being sold back to us. We live in a world where in many developed countries more people will vote in reality TV show talent quests than in the presidential election of their country. We find people shedding the old idea of citizenship, whereby people contributed and had responsibility and connection to others. In its place is consumerism, wherein people are owed and entitled and are the center of all rights and authority.

THE TROUBLE WITH PARIS

I am at a crowded party in an inner-city apartment. People are squashed wall to wall. I find myself talking to a young woman. She shares with me that despite her good job and great friends, she feels unhappy. I ask her what she means by "unhappy." She tells me that she has lost focus in life; she wakes up lethargic and finds herself crying a lot for seemingly no reason. My pastoral training tells me that this girl is suffering from a case of depression. I begin to ask some gentle, probing questions about the rest of her life. She tells me that she thinks she is in this state because she has become stale. She has been living in the same house now for three years, and it is time to move on. She is fed up with her job and wants a change. Her solution to the problem is to move to Paris to freshen up her life. She feels as if she needs to *experience* something new.

I ask her what her parents think of the move. She has stopped talking to her mother, she tells me. I ask her why, and she discloses that three months ago her mother left her father for a family friend. Her father was not coping; suddenly the real problem that was causing this girl's depression had surfaced. Still, the young woman was unable to see it. She was convinced that she would be happy when she got to Paris. All she had to do was travel and find new friends and a new job to *experience* life as it was meant to be—exciting, stimulating, and meaningful.

Six months later I receive an e-mail message from this girl. She was now in Ireland; Paris was not all she had expected. If only I had a dollar for every time I had a conversation like this. Her story was typical of coming of age in a time when we are told to find meaning through accumulating experiences.

A WORLD OF MICROPLEASURES

Life as it is presented to many young adults by the hyper-consumer world is a never-ending array of pleasures and experiences to enjoy. No longer do we look for big dreams to shape our lives; instead, we prefer to chase the experience. Anything that could curtail this chase, be it commitment, a mortgage, marriage, or family, must be dropped in the relentless pursuit of new and stimulating experiences. We must feel good to feel as if we have lives of significance. Gone are the questions of the past: How do I deal with the burden of sin? How do I become reconnected with God? The contemporary person does not seek salvation in the way Christians have understood it for the last two thousand years. Instead, people seek to find meaning in "feeling good" in the moment. This fact is pointed out by cultural critic Christopher Lasch: "The contemporary climate is . . . not religious. People today hunger not for personal salvation . . . but for the feeling, the momentary illusion, of personal well-being."[3]

Young people have almost completely given up on the idea of a future. Ask your friends what they will be doing in five years, and you will receive blank stares. We do know, however, what people will be doing in five years: they will be chasing experiences. It could be the lure of travel, the hunt for the ultimate sexual encounter, the once-in-a-lifetime concert, the most stimulating workplace, the best Tahitian massage, or the most insane bungee jump. Today's youth have been programmed to find meaning in experience and are slaves to this framework.

The chase of the experience is often pitched as noble, as countercultural; purchasers of the experience see themselves as turning their backs on materialism. This could not be further from the truth. The hyperconsumer culture is shifting our focus from buying tangible items that exist in time and space and instead encouraging us to buy experiences that are liquid and fleeting and that require no production or factories and thus are cheaper for corporations to produce. Jeremy Rifkin, founder and president of the Foundation on Economic Trends, describes this shift:

> We are making a long-term shift from industrial production to cultural production. More and more cutting-edge commerce in the future will involve the marketing of a vast

array of cultural experiences rather than of just traditional industrial-based goods and services. Global travel and tourism, theme cities and parks, destination entertainment centers, wellness, fashion and cuisine, professional sports and games, gambling, music, film, television, the virtual worlds of cyberspace, and electronically mediated entertainment of every kind are fast becoming the center of a new hypercapitalism that trades in access to cultural experiences.[4]

We are encouraged to chase experiences because it is cheaper for our economy to produce experiences that need no production or factories to create them. The hyperconsumer world prefers that we spend our pay instantly instead of saving it. It prefers that we spend our money on travel rather than real estate, as our hard-earned money is then placed straight back into the economy.

We are sold the myth that it is through the consumption of these packaged experiences that we will find status, social connection, and ultimately meaning. Just look at the almost religious emphasis our culture puts on travel. We are told that we "must do Italy," that we must "broaden our horizons." No one raises an eyebrow when the average young adult spends tens of thousands of dollars chasing "experiences" that we are told are invaluable, when the reality is that we return from the same well-worn tourist paths with only photos, some fleeting memories, and a massive credit card bill. When people don't think or plan for the future, they spend in the moment.

This is a pattern of behavior that has been carefully shaped in young adults by those who have the most to gain from hyper-consumer culture. Among many young adults, experience becomes a way of gaining status. Those who have had more exotic and exclusive experiences find themselves at the top of the social pile. Those who cannot afford such purchases are told they "need to get out more and experience the world and stop being so boring."

Property is now sold to young adults on the merits of the experience that it can deliver. We are told to buy in this hip inner-city neighborhood because it is near the "experience zones" of cafés and clubs, or so that we can "experience" its bohemian culture. The function of the dwelling almost becomes irrelevant compared to the social status it can deliver its owner in the experience economy. Even religion can be subverted as the spiritual shopper searches for the latest experience to offer momentary and fleeting satisfaction. Once the experience is attained, it is consumed. The seeker then moves on to another aisle in the religious supermarket to find another experience to sample.

The reality is that as soon as we purchase an experience, it is gone and we need another hit in order to be satisfied. We find ourselves on a treadmill seeking out new experiences that leave us adrift and disconnected, constantly dissatisfied yet continuing to center our lives around the unrelenting sampling of packaged experiences—a sampling that leaves us wanting to be saved in the future by the "romance of when," yet eternally stuck in the present.

IN THE MOMENT

When life becomes a never-ending chase for experiences and pleasurable moments, the way we view time will inevitably change. The past now seems to exist only as an inspiration for retro fashion, and the future is either an apocalyptic dystopia or a technological utopia, depending on our mood. All that matters is the present. Hyperconsumer culture does not want us to think about the future, just as the fast-food supplier does not want us to think of the future ramifications of the fat-laden snack we are about to buy. Rather, they want us to think only in the moment, focusing on immediate gratification.

When we think about the future, we are inevitably faced with consequences—consequences that will often mean we don't make the purchase for which advertisers exist. When I ask groups of young adults about the plans for their future, I find they can't even think five years ahead. Thinking of the future jeopardizes the safe bubble of living in the present. Consumers don't consider being patient. The idea of saving up to make a purchase is passé in a credit card culture where we can have it all and we can have it now.

Microwave ovens were an invention that incredibly sped up the cooking process. Now, however, we often find ourselves becoming impatient and counting down the clock. Two minutes seems an eternity to wait for our food to be heated. Our expectations of instant gratification grow as technology is able to deliver us things more and more quickly. Therefore the hyperreal world has not only inflated our expectations of what life can offer us, it has told us that this wonderful life is just around the corner and that we don't have to wait. If we do have to wait, that is evidence that what we thought we wanted is not worth waiting for, so we instinctively move on to the next thing. More and more, hyperreality begins to look like a modern-day religion.

FOUR

Hyperconsumerism
As Religion

In the last several years, we have seen advertisers not only apply layers of meaning to our innate human needs, such as sex, but also to our spiritual needs for transcendence and love. We find some marketers fooling themselves into believing that they can actually take over the roles that religion, relationships, and even love play in life. Just listen to top advertising executive Kevin Roberts as he advises his peers in business and marketing:

> What if we could use the same idea to account for people's passionate devotion to . . . religions? To small local businesses as well as global brands, events as well as intimate experiences? What if forming long-term emotional relationships could be more than a catchphrase? What if brands could grow and evolve with richer and deeper connections in the same way that people can in their lives? What if the emotion that could make this transformation was love?[1]

Sadly, Roberts is not joking. Take a look at his Web site, and you will see that it is filled with people who claim deep emotional connections with products and brands. As one advertisement for sunglasses I saw said, "Girlfriends may come and go, but I will always have my sunglasses." Wow, monogamy is out except when it comes to products. Thus, for many, consumption becomes a way of filling the void in our lives that comes from not being able to get what we really want.

Often when I am speaking to groups about consumerism, I ask people to raise their hands if they have ever made a purchase when they were feeling down. Almost without exception, 90 percent of the group confesses that they have engaged in retail therapy. No longer do we look just to the spiritual to give us solace. For the religious age has passed and the age of consumerism as religion is upon us. Cultural commentators Helen Trinca and Catherine Fox note:

> For many of us, buying the goods and services we want does wonders psychologically. When we spend, we see the rewards of our hard work. Once those rewards were more abstract. We may have felt happy that we were doing our duty to God or our community, or enjoyed the feeling that work was itself a virtuous activity, a good thing to do. Our reward for work was financial but also spiritual or religious. Materialism, hedonism, the linking of happiness with consumption were all regarded as dubious pursuits in a religious age. . . . Consumption has filled the vacuum of meaning in the twenty-first century and plays a powerful role in our

ambitions. You may not get an interesting job—after all, not everyone can—but you can moderate the anger and sadness at missing out by buying hard, by acquiring goods that describe you and how you live your life.[2]

As our Western culture has moved away from the religious and spiritual beliefs that have given us solace, meaning, and direction, we have not necessarily stopped acting religiously. For evidence of this, all you have to do is go to a sporting event, or notice the way people get teary-eyed when they hear their national anthem, or watch the way we make pilgrimage to inventory sales, or note how many people expect the overseas vacation to an exotic land to make them better people. Hyperconsumerism fits as the perfect religion of our age. The real killer is that all of this is occurring at a soul level, an emotional level. We are oblivious to this effect upon our lives. But it is deep down in our hearts, guts, and groins that advertising grabs us. That is why experts describe these new religions of the secular West as "implicit religions," meaning that they are unspoken or unnamed religions. In the absence of an active, soul-filled, emotionally connected faith, we have resorted to another kind. We worship at the mall, buying products as if they were magic amulets; we place our hope and faith in vacations and SUVs to make us happy; and we work and save and borrow to reach the consumer version of heaven—the lifestyle we dream about. Peter Brierley says of implicit religion, "It is emotional rather than logical, felt rather than reasoned. It is personal not impersonal, and thus individualized, consistent with a postmodern world."[3] Thus we have no defense, because we don't know that we are being attacked; we worship without realizing that we have made a new faith commitment.

Secular culture has pushed faith into the private sphere, making it something to be practiced behind closed doors. Thus religion has been robbed of its power to change the individual and culture. In the absence of religious belief that has the impetus to change culture, hyperconsumerism acts as a sort of "religion lite," simply serving our emotional state. Religious rituals and beliefs are subverted and made impotent by the consumer culture and turned into marketable products, such as religious symbols worn by those who see them simply as fashion items that have nothing to do with their original meaning.

Therefore, the symbols and practices that stood as anchors in culture, offering guidance, solace, and authority, have now been weakened. They have been reduced to mere products, able to be used by the purchasers in whatever ways they like. The ultimate authority and religion remains the consumer culture. Look at what your hope is in. There you will find your true religion. Theologian Lesslie Newbigin defined religion as

> that which has final authority for a believer or a society, both in the sense that it determines one's scale of values and in the sense that it provides the models, the basic patterns through which the believer grasps and organizes his or her experience. . . . It also becomes necessary to point out that what someone calls "their religion" may in fact be other than the ultimately authoritative factor in their thinking and acting.[4]

Realizing that what we *say* is our religion may not actually *be* our religion is a devastating realization. We have swapped a biblical worldview that places our hope in a God who is active in our world for the seemingly immediate and tangible worldview of hyperconsumerism. We keep our faith lives in the back of the closet to pull out on Sundays. Hyperconsumerism is what we really place our faith in to deliver a meaningful and fulfilled life in the here and now. Just look at the way in which the message of the church has become subverted by hyperconsumerism. Today's salvation message sounds more like "self-help" than "die to self." For many, the gospel becomes a vehicle to deliver the good life promised by hyperconsumerism.

Hyperconsumerism has infiltrated our culture and lives in such a way that we no longer notice it. It is now the primary operating system that we look to for a fulfilling life. If we are to define religion as the worldview and beliefs that determine our identity, actions, and hope, then hyperconsumerism is the biggest church in town. Sadly, we find Christianity relegated to just another consumer choice, another lifestyle option. The Christian becomes like the Italian cuisine aficionado, the *Star Trek* fan, or the snowboarder. The all-encompassing power of the gospel message is neutered by consumer culture. Dallas Willard explains: "We now live in a time when consumer Christianity has become the accepted norm, and all-out engagement with and in Jesus' kingdom among us is regarded as just one option people may take if it suits them—but probably as somewhat 'overdoing it.'"[5]

The implicit religion of hyperconsumerism contains many of

the echoes of Christian faith. Malls and movie theaters resemble churches. Celebrities resemble saints. Shopping becomes a sacrament, and gossip magazines become scripture. Even conversion takes on a new form in the hyperconsumer world. In the hyperreal world, we believe that by changing our surfaces we are undergoing conversion.

SURFACE OBSESSIONS

The more our spirituality becomes about buying products and experiences, the more we become obsessed by image and surface. The politician who looks younger and more virile will win out over a rival who may be a better leader but who is not photogenic. We prefer the sexy pop star with a carefully marketed attitude to the musician who can sing but is not good looking. We will pay more for the mustard that comes in an exotic-looking jar with a foreign name than for the cheaper and possibly tastier local variety.

As we value things that are material, we become less and less interested in the interior life of things or people. John Kavanaugh explains: "The more we try to ground our identities in external possessions or triumphs, the more we plaster our names on everything we can accumulate, the more we cling to surface and style, the less we find underneath."[6] Hyperconsumerism turns everything into a product. We ourselves become products, but for products to be "buyable," they must have good packaging. If we don't have good packaging, we risk becoming an "irrelevant" product that no one wants to buy.

ME AS BRAND

I am looking at a random personal Web page on a social net-working Web site. In case you have been stuck in the Russian space station for the last few years, social networking Web sites, primarily for young people—such as MySpace, Facebook, and Bebo—have taken our culture by storm. The young man's Web page I have chosen to look at is fairly typical. Smack bang in the middle of his page is a picture of him and his girlfriend. There is nothing unusual about a twenty-four-year-old male romantically displaying a picture of his special lady. But this photo is different. The first thing that hits me is just how big the picture is—it dwarfs everything else on his page. Okay, I lie; the thing that hits me about the picture is this: how did such an ordinary-looking guy get a girlfriend who looks like *that*? Looking at the smug expression on the guy's face and noticing the way he holds his girlfriend like a trophy, I realize that this picture is not about romance; it is about social status.

Next is a picture of his brand-new BMW sedan, which is followed by a picture of his hip-looking apartment. As I scroll down his page, I find at least ten other pictures of this guy at nightclubs and parties with a variety of people who are cool or attractive or a combination of both. The page is a thinly dis-guised attempt by this young man to show that he is a social success. Despite what millions of social networking Web site users will tell you, the network is not about catching up with friends or blogging (keeping an online diary), but rather about social status within the new media environment. The key cultural currency on social networking Web sites is the number of people who have registered themselves on your personal page as your "friends." Knowing someone is not a prerequisite to registering yourself as his or her "friend." All you have to do is click on a few icons and list yourself as a friend. Spend a short time on social networking Web sites, and you will realize that they are a sort of giant Generation-Y social version of the Hindu caste system.

To achieve a high ranking of "friends," you need to have the following equation in your favor: Your personal hotness + your coolness + buying the right music + choosing the right TV and DVDs to watch + making the right travel choices + appearing to be socially busy + engaging in cool hobbies/interests = high friends ranking.

A social networking Web site is a way for young people who have come of age in a media-saturated environment to position themselves and to establish identity. In a media environment in which marketing is king, young people have become marketers of their own personal image and "brand." A giant onus then comes upon them: it is up to them to create a package of purchases that communicates the right messages to those around them about who they are. If they chose the right consumer choices, they are lauded as cool, stylish, hip, cosmopolitan, tasteful, or classy. If they make the wrong choices, they become embarrassing, tacky, distasteful, dorky, and worst of all, uncool.

This pressure to measure up adds to people's anxiety. It is as if they are now products and must market, advertise, and sell themselves. And if they are now brands and products, what happens when they go out of style? Thus they are trapped in a gargantuan struggle to remain attractive, cool, funny, sexy, and smart in order to remain relevant to friends and peers. What happens when they age? What does this sort of worldview say to those who are not attractive or do not fit the mold? It says to them that they are worthless unless they can begin the hyper-consumer culture version of spiritual conversion, the makeover.

MAKEOVER

I often talk to groups of young adults about the monastic move-ment of the Middle Ages, when young people all over medieval Europe left their secular lives to take vows of self-denial and join orders. I tell of how monks and nuns would rise early in the morning to engage in all kinds of spiritual disciplines and exer-cises. To most young adults today, the idea of rising early in the morning to engage in spiritual discipline is a foreign concept. The idea of committing yourself to such a task seems almost impossible in our secular age. Yet get up early and drive your car around your neighborhood and you will find young adults run-ning and jogging early in the morning. They will be sweating, struggling, and pushing past the pain barrier. Go to the gym, and there you will find young adults exerting, groaning, pulling, and straining, all while paying for the privilege. Go to your local beauty salon, and there you will find twenty- and thirtysome-thing females (and occasionally males), being preened, plucked, buffed, tanned, and waxed. Stick your head into the tattoo parlor, and you will find the members of the supposedly noncommittal generation being branded for posterity. Head to the mall, and you will find more young adults handing over hard-earned cash for clothes, styling wands, hair gel, and luxury handbags. Nothing has changed since the Middle Ages; we still get up early and commit ourselves to improvement. The only difference is that the monks and nuns were attempting to change their internal spiritual lives, while today we believe in conversion and salvation through changing the exteriors of ourselves and the things we own. We see this theme played out again and again on reality television and in the press coverage of Hollywood stars who lose weight and tone up, thus rejuvenating their careers. No longer do we look to be spiritually reborn; we just need a makeover, to be restyled and touched up.

I recently watched a reality makeover show. The woman who had been selected for a makeover had being trying to have a baby for several years, only to suffer a number of miscarriages. The woman had finally successfully given birth to a healthy child, only for that child to tragically die in its first year of life. The show lavished the woman with various makeovers. They remodeled her house and her garden, taught her how to cook gourmet dishes, helped her lose weight, and gave her a new wardrobe of the latest fashions, along with a European vacation. The show ended in an almost awkward fashion as it become apparent that the world of makeovers could never heal this woman's grief. Her problems were internal, not external, and our culture had no solution for her pain.

We no longer value the person who is kind, caring, honest, or patient. Sure, we may offer these qualities lip service, but the reality is that our culture worships how we look on the outside. Our character runs second to our exterior. The common belief is that if we can change our outsides, we will change our insides. Our obsession with changing ourselves gives away another trait of the hyperreal world, radical individualism. We are told by the hyperreal culture that in order to have lives of meaning, we must be focused on ourselves and our needs.

FIVE

It's All About You!

One of the reasons that both hyperreality and hyper-consumerism have such a stranglehold on our imaginations is that our culture is based on worship of the individual. We have all grown up with stories that revolve around the individual who, despite all the odds, believes in his or her dream and makes it to the top. It could be the ballerina, the rapper, the businessman, or the politician. We are obsessed with the concept of the individual "making it." These stories of other people making it fuel our desire to make it ourselves. Echoing through TV programs, award shows, and all forms of popular culture, we hear the contemporary commandments telling us how to live.

The underlying message seems to be clear: success, a happy life, meaning, or even the chance to become a celebrity is just over the horizon for individuals who want it enough. It is almost unthinkable to us as Western people that in other parts of the world people place their families or communities above their own desires and wants. We are so ingrained with individualism that we cannot imagine any other way to live. As our culture progresses to a more consumerist framework, we are becoming even more focused on the individual. The individual—his needs, his rights, and his wants—becomes the central point around which our society arranges itself. The modern individual becomes the one who discovers truth, the one who makes himself successful in our economic world by achieving career goals and by reaching a standard of living and comfort by buying the right products.

I recently drove past a billboard that pictured a young man with Down syndrome. The advertisement featured all of the young man's achievements at the Special Olympics and encouraged the reader not to judge the disabled, making the point that disabled people can be successful in their endeavors just like everyone else. On one hand the message was right: disabled people can be high achievers just like those of us who happen not to be disabled; but on the other hand, the advertisement revealed our cultural fixation on individual achievement. What about all of those people out there, both disabled and not disabled, who are not achieving—are they not worthy people? You will never see a billboard celebrating a person because he or she is a kind or noble person. No, we are addicted to the idea of our individual worth being linked to our achievements. The person who is seen as being a nonachiever in our culture will often be called a "loser," which gives away the fact that we see our lives as a game of achievement. In our culture of personal freedom, we are told that we will find meaning through what we do.

Not only are we meant to find meaning in what we do in terms of vocation and achievement, but we are meant to find happiness through choosing the right pleasurable pursuits. Our culture tells us that if we as individuals can manage to achieve all of this, then we will be happy. What an incredible burden!

I must decide if I believe there is a God. I must decide how to live. I must achieve. I must find the right combination of things to enjoy to find happiness. And I must find the solutions to the pain and suffering life brings. I must make myself lovable, attractive, and interesting to connect with those who will then provide me with love, sex, intimacy, affection, and support.

I remember an advertisement that featured thousands of people trying to form a human pyramid. The pyramid was so huge that it grew bigger than the buildings around it, yet people were falling off and pulling each other down in an effort to reach the top. In many ways this is what the culture of individualism does to us. The cost can be catastrophic upon our sense of community and civic responsibility. Individualism carries with its sense of personal freedom a heavy cost, as missiologist Duane Elmer illuminates:

> Whenever individualism reigns supreme, community is easily sacrificed for personal preferences. Although I enjoy the luxuries of individualism, I cannot help but feel that it has also brought a certain impoverishment. Too quickly we splinter churches, friendships, families, and groups rather than struggle for ways to bridge differences, reconnect, forgive, reconcile, and heal. Individualism fosters an impatience with people and institutions; we can always join another church, find new friends, or get another job.[1]

Yet the habit of individualism is hard to kick. We like to have the freedom of individualism, yet we desire the consolation of relationships. We find it hard to give up on the individualist dream of making it to the top, of getting that good life. Many of us know no other way. It is the only story we have ever heard. We are told from childhood that with grit and determination and a bit of good fortune, we can have a happy life. But as life goes on, we realize that we are not, as individuals, in control, and that circumstance and reality fight against the myths of our childhood. Sure, we may see ourselves as sitting on the throne of individualism, but real life tells us that we are not in control. One evidence of this truth is the fact that we age, and contemporary culture therefore finds itself obsessed with the denial of aging and the worship of youth.

ADULESCENCE

Hyperconsumer culture is turning into a massive youth culture, a society in which being young is an attitude, not an age. Welcome to the world of the *twixters*. In Japan they are called *freeters*, in other countries *Peter Pans*; and they are changing our culture. Twixters are young adults who range in age from the late teens to midthirties. They live in a permanent in-between stage of life. They move from job to job and see themselves as part of youth culture. Romantic and sexual relationships to them are fluid and nonbinding, except when it comes to their connections with their parents, with whom they often share a codependent relationship. They spend most of their money on music, fashion, travel, and entertainment. Their peers are everything to them, and if they are going to get married at all, they will do it late in life. For most twixters, marriage and children change very little of their desire to be part of youth culture.

Married twixters are terrified by the enormity of their commitment, and many see no moral issue with text-flirting with people who are not their spouses. They turn child rearing into a consumer exercise in social competition. Twixter families are not like *Leave It to Beaver*. Dad is on the video game console while looking after the kids, and Mom, like a desperate housewife, is pounding the pavement to get back her prebaby figure to fit into those skintight jeans she saw on sale last week. There are already twixters in their forties, and all trends are pointing to the fact that they are not going to grow up—ever!

Even the baby boomers are getting in on the act. The middle-aged are "living it up" before they move into their twilight years. They are spending their children's inheritance on iPods, plasma TVs, and travel. Empty nesters ironically are moving to the same hip inner-city neighborhoods as their children, not because they want to be close to their kids, but just for the coffee. Companies make millions from selling a youthful rebel dream to the middle-aged. Middle-aged divorcées reinvent themselves with hip new outfits and attitudes. The Rolling Stones still sell out stadiums even though they are in their sixties. English demographers are shocked by the numbers of people in their fifties taking up smoking, binge drinking, and night clubbing. It seems that thirty is the new twenty, forty is the new thirty, sixty is the new fifty, and so on—you get the picture!

Hyperconsumer culture is a culture that worships youth. This is also the reason, however, that so many young adults fear aging. Aging and death are the spotlights that illuminate the fraudulence of the hyperreal culture's promises to deliver us a good life. Hyperreal culture has no answer for the ticking hands of time. All it can do is distract us from the facts that we age, we feel pain, and we are going to die. Sadly, our self-obsessed culture, with its fixation on youth, has deeply changed how we relate to one another. A focus on the individual mixed with a hyperconsumer worldview has changed how we view human relationships and commitment.

LIFE AS A CELL-PHONE CONTRACT

Hyperconsumerism has deeply affected how we view human relationships and commitment. The ways in which humans have shown commitment, loyalty, and community over the last several thousand years have been radically altered in our lifetime. This change in the way we view commitment is further evidence of the way the framework of consumerism is influencing the whole of our lives. When my dad became a Christian as a young adult, he did not know all the "rules" that dominated the 1960s conservative culture. After his sudden conversion, he had been attending a local church. He asked some of his new Christian friends along to the movies to see the latest Pink Panther film. Without realizing it, he had broken one of the key rules of the 1960s Christian ghetto—going to the movies. The church elders found out, and swift action was taken to ensure that such a terrible occurrence would not happen again. Good Christians were not to attend such worldly venues such as cinemas; leaders asked of their young people, "How will you feel if when Jesus returns he finds you in a cinema?"

One man told me the story of his struggle with an idea that had been put in his head as a young boy by way of a sermon. The pastor delivering the sermon had said that after each person's death, God would play back the whole of his or her life in front of friends and family. Another young woman told me that in her church the young women were encouraged to tape down their nipples before they entered church so as not to tempt the young men into sexual lust. Such ideas were based on a view of God as a sort of cosmic judge or policeman who was sitting in the heavens with a giant stick ready to whack us the minute we stepped out of line. When we look at Western culture, we see that this view of God and faith was very much influenced by cultures run by emperors, kings, and queens in times when God's representatives on earth could chop off the heads of those who stepped out of line. On the whole, this view of a controlling God has become passé. In its place, a new view of faith has taken hold in the lives of Christians.

CONTRACTUAL FAITH

For most people living in the postindustrial world, our lives are determined not by a framework of control but by contract. Now, I don't want you to think of a mahogany-paneled lawyer's office filled with books and dusty parchments. Instead, think of a cell phone contract. When I enter the cell phone dealer's store, I come with an agenda. I want to get the best phone I can get while paying the least amount for the service. The cell phone salesperson has her own agenda; she wants to sign me up for the longest, most expensive contract possible. She will promise me all kinds of features, such as video and conference calling, deals, plans, covers, and accessories, to lure me into thinking that I have made a good deal. Basically, I want the best results by putting forth the minimum effort. This sort of contract has become one of the main frameworks in which we view life, for technologies such as cell phones are never neutral; they always have a social effect.

The combination of new technologies with a hyper-consumer culture is powerfully changing the way we relate to each other. Cell phones and the Internet allow us to communicate more, but they also allow us to communicate in more superficial ways. Instead of having to spend quality time with our loved ones, we can now text message them a short communication from work. We can live away from our families with the excuse of being able to look at them through a pixel-ated webcam. The age of cheap airline travel means we can change cities with the excuse of cheap flights home. Technology's promise of creating better ways of connecting actually ends up diminishing our ability to live in deep, connected relationships. But despite the nagging feelings of loneliness we feel, we are rarely aware of the way we now view relationships. We have grown up knowing nothing else. Most young adults have grown up as a generation that has, through advertising, been targeted by corporations since birth. We have been taught from a very early age to look for the best deal in order to be great shoppers.

Thus we have become saturated with this view that makes us treat life as a contractual negotiation. We enter into contract-like agreements with our governments, families, partners, employers, and even our churches. I recently heard of an emerging trend where people make a list of their friends and divide them into an A group and a B group. The A group includes the friends whom they "get a lot out of," and the B group lists the friends that are more hard work than fun, the people who tend to require more emotional investment. You make appointments with—or if you cannot be bothered, you text or e-mail—the people on the B list, telling them that you do not want to be friends with them anymore. At first this trend seems strange, but just think about the way our culture has let hyperconsumerism influence our sexuality. The television series *Sex and the City* illuminates the way we now view sexuality as a consumer exchange. The men that the stars of the show become involved with sexually are spoken about in the same terms as the high-fashion products the girls lust after. Our culture has totally subverted sexuality within the framework of contract. When it comes to sex, love is dead, and shopping rules.

It is not just sexuality that is subverted by hyperconsumerism. While many young people still join the military to serve their country, one only has to observe advertising campaigns for the military that promise all kinds of benefits for enlisting: friendship, fitness, self-actualization, and education are all goodies on offer. The military offers the potential recruit a contractual understanding of serving their country. The age when the young would join to give their lives for their country out of patriotic servanthood now lies only in dusty history books. They are given the chance to serve their country, but the primary benefit on offer is self-actualization. It is almost as if John F. Kennedy's words, "Ask not what your country can do for you, but what you can do for your country," have been reversed, with government becoming the servant of the individual's rights, lifestyle, and wealth accumulation. The idea of giving one's life for a higher cause has become alien to most in the Western culture. This was made evident by the events of September 11, 2001, when many Western people showed great shock at the willingness of suicide bombers to give their lives for the cause of radical Islam. In fact, Al Qaeda took inspiration in the fact that although they were militarily outgunned by the West, they were willing to give their lives for the struggle, whereas Western people were not.

Albeit misguided, the conviction and dedication shown by groups such as Al Qaeda are totally absent in hyperconsumer culture. We are incapable of such dedication because we are afraid to commit, to put our stakes in the ground, because to do so means we could miss out. The cell phone contract worldview tells us, "Don't get stuck in a relationship. Even though the person you are with is attractive, someone better could be just around the corner. Somewhere there are better friends, better sex, a better experience, and a better product, so don't get tied down. Relationships and commitment limit your options." As sociologist Zygmunt Bauman shows us, our hyperconsumer culture constantly tells us, "Don't let yourself be caught. Avoid embraces that are too tight. Remember, the deeper and denser your attachments, commitments, engagements, the greater your risk."[2]

We run from those promises and covenants that humans have made to each other for thousands of years because they frighten us to death. Many today fear such commitment-based social institutions because self now takes precedence over commitment. As the worldview of hyperconsumerism has taken hold of our imaginations, everything has become shopping. We must not become entangled in commitments, because they could limit our options on finding something better. This constant search for something better means that the supershoppers of hyperconsumerism are still waiting for a better deal after the mall has closed and then are forced to return home empty-handed. Or we find ourselves always on the move, searching for a home that shifts and shimmies over the horizon. We keep up this restlessness as our fears of not being stimulated take over.

The key to life, we are told, is to keep holding out for that perfect bargain. But the less we commit, the more we become passive. We never make a move; instead, we simply stand and watch life go by. Our fear of commitment has turned us into passive consumers. We have become voyeurs, watching other people have a life. Pornography shows us other people having sex; gossip magazines show us the emotional lives of celebrities; nature documentaries show us the natural world while we sit in our artificial lounge rooms; reality TV shows us the lives of ordinary people; lifestyle programs show us others doing domestic work; sports teams show us others playing; chat shows show us others conversing. We have stopped having "real" lives; instead, we live hyperreal zombielike lives, remaining uncommitted and out of touch with the art of actual living.

Our commitment phobia is limiting our ability to truly enjoy life. How then are we to find a way out of hyperreality? How are we to find a way in which to live as a culture that is not trapped by the promises of hyperreal culture? Quite simply, consumerism has invaded every part of our consciousness. If we are to reclaim our freedom, we cannot simply buy our way out of the hyperconsumerist world. If we are to avoid the alluring yet imprisoning temptations of the hyperreal condition, we must effect a different kind of revolution—a revolution that begins with the human heart. But before we can effect a revolution, we must leave the world of hyperreality and make a stop off at the world of reality.

Part 2

Reality

SIX

How Hyperreality
Makes Us Unhappy

All we have to do is peel back the veneer of the hyperreal world to find the rot underneath. We have to ask hard questions, such as, "Is the way we are living going to deliver the abundant life Jesus offered in John 10:10?" If we are to live with meaning and fulfillment, if we are to be people of dynamic and relevant faith, we must deconstruct the mythic promises of the hyperreal world. For those of us who call ourselves followers of Jesus, getting help dealing with the problems that affect our happiness here on earth and that are so deeply linked to our faith can prove a futile search. Sadly, many of us have even given up on our faith contributing to any betterment of our life here on earth. Sure, we look forward to heaven, but how do we live here and now? Well, before we find out how following Jesus can make our lives meaningful, connected, and satisfying here on earth, we need to examine how the myths of the hyperreal world can ruin our lives.

CHOPPING DOWN THE TREES OF HYPERREALITY

As we confront hyperreality, we can learn from the story of the early English missionary Boniface (also known as Winfried). Boniface was born in Devonshire around the end of the seventh century. As a young man, he felt a call to share the gospel with the pagan Germanic tribes of the Rhineland. These tribes had originally turned to Christianity but had reverted to their pagan beliefs. The tribes' belief system was centered around the idea of trees—sacred oaks, to be precise—as idols. Such a powerful framework of belief needed radical action. Boniface came up with a controversial (if not highly politically incorrect) yet extremely effective strategy to deal with the Germanic pagan worldview. Author and speaker Ruth Tucker tells the following story:

> Many of the so-called Christians of the area had reverted to paganistic practices . . . and were involved in spirit worship and magical arts. To counteract this sacrilege Boniface was convinced drastic measures were needed, so he boldly struck a blow to the very heart of the local pagan worship. He assembled a large crowd at Geismar, where the sacred oak of the Thundergod was located, and with the people looking on in horror he began chopping down the tree. It was a defiant act, but one that clearly drew attention to the fact that there was no supernatural power in either the tree or the god whom it honored.[1]

Later in life Boniface began to question his confrontational model of dealing with the belief systems of the people with whom he was doing ministry. The more culturally sensitive methods of his peers, the Celtic missionaries, turned out to be far more successful. Nevertheless, Boniface's story is important for us. I am not suggesting that we head off to the local temple or shopping mall with ax in hand; rather, I believe we need to apply Boniface's strategy to the sacred oak of hyperreality in our own heart. We need to begin chopping away at the tree that has taken root in our imaginations. The journey is often painful and confrontational, but it is the beginning of the road to freedom. So sharpen that ax, and let's start chopping.

HAPPINESS STUDIES/WELL-BEING/DEPRESSION

One of the young adults I mentored recently told me a story about his friend from college. His friend had come into his university course and almost instantly become one of the most popular students. He had the right hip look and personality, and he excelled at his studies. After graduation he was able to score a top job in his industry, where he continued to excel in his field, and then he moved to take up an important position in Europe. With weekend jaunts to the top vacation spots across Europe, a glamorous job, and a great social life, he had become the envy of his peers. His peers, however, could barely believe it when he returned home to his parents and decided that his only option, despite just reaching his mid-twenties, was to commit suicide. Sadly, this is not an isolated incident; suicide is a chronic issue in developed first world countries.

The flip side of this time of great economic comfort is that beneath the shiny, happy surface of hyperreal culture lies a murky swamp of anxiety and depression. Despite all of the material privilege, technological advancement, employment opportunities, and entertainment options we possess, an incredible number of us are experiencing depression as never before. In fact, the number of young adults who are experiencing depression is staggering. "One recently completed study of Generation-Y'ers, conducted by researchers at Simmons College (Mass.), found that fully one-third of them had 'succumbed to depression' by age 27."[2] Despite our material comfort, we are no happier; in fact, we are more depressed, as psychologist David Myers explains:

> Today's 25-year-olds are much more likely to recall a time in their lives when they were despondent and despairing than are their 75-year-old grandparents, despite the grandparents having had many more years to suffer all kinds of disorders, from broken legs to the anguish of depression. Similar trends are evident in Canada, Sweden, Germany, and New Zealand. Everywhere in the modern world, it seems, more younger adults than older adults report having ever been disabled by this new great (emotional) depression . . . Young people today have grown up with much more affluence, slightly less overall happiness, and much greater risk of depression, not to mention triple suicide . . . Never has a culture experienced such physical comfort combined with such psychological misery.[3]

Surely this information flies in the face of the message we are given every day, that by purchasing more, consuming more, and having more money at our disposal, we will be happier. Not so. If we were starving in a poor African village, there is no doubt having more money would make us happier, for it would mean that we would be able to purchase much needed food for ourselves and our loved ones. However, when the whole of a society gets richer, we become none the happier. Well-being expert Richard Layard comments on what the research is telling us: "Extra income is really valuable when it lifts people away from sheer physical poverty. This corresponds to one of the key beliefs of the nineteenth-century economists—that the extra happiness provided by extra income is greatest when you are poor, and then declines steadily as you get richer."[4] This is a stunning revelation that has deep consequences for how our culture views the attainment of a good life. Stop and think for a second—this evidence goes against almost everything you have been told since you were born. This is the stuff you wish you knew long ago. Put quite simply, unless you are desperately poor, more money is not going to contribute at all to your sense of happiness.

This reality has radical implications for how we arrange our priorities, our time, and our vocations. Sadly, despite what secular social scientists are telling us about the link between wealth and happiness, the global situation is not changing. The poorest people on our planet need more money, and those who are in the developed world will be no happier if they gain more money. Yet the opposite reality is true: the poorest people in our world continue to get poorer while the boom economy of the West continues to provide those who already have so much with even more. Layard continues, "So we have in the First World a deep paradox—a society that seeks and delivers ever greater income, but is little if any happier than before. At the same time in the Third World, where extra income really does bring extra happiness, income levels are still very low. And the First World has more depression, more alcoholism, and more crime than fifty years ago. What is going on?"[5]

What is going on is that Boniface's ax is slamming into the sacred oak of hyperreality, for the hyperreal world is based on our dissatisfaction. People make money off of you due to your feeling inadequate, unhappy, and unsatisfied. This is kind of like going on a vacation and putting an ad in the local prison advertising for house sitters. We are entrusting the task of making our lives happy into the hands of a corporate culture that has a vested interest in keeping us unhappy.

So no matter how affluent or comfortable our lives become, we will always be looking ahead for something better. In many ways this "I will be happy when . . ." culture is the ultimate "addiction" culture, as people enter the addictive downward spiral, always needing a bigger hit to satisfy their growing cravings and becoming less free in the process. Our entire economy has moved away from making things that "serve" us to making us dissatisfied until we buy things we don't need. The entire media culture that we are immersed in each day is dedicated to keeping us dissatisfied. The unhappier we are, the more we will buy. The hyperreal culture severely harms your chances of having a happy and fulfilling life. But why is this so? How could the messages we have heard all our lives about what makes a good life be so wrong? One reason is that constantly comparing ourselves and what we own and do with others makes us unhappy.

COMPARISON ANXIETY

I was about twenty minutes into delivering the keynote speech at a large church's young adult camp when I suddenly stopped midsentence. I saw something that I had to call the group's attention to. Ever since I had arrived at the event, I sensed that something was not right with the young women in the room. The sense of competition among the young women was almost palpable. I could see the cliques, the outsiders, and the "in" group. The males in the room were almost irrelevant in this social power struggle based on popularity and comparison. I told the group that I was concerned with what I was observing: this was supposed to be the body of Christ in which everyone was accepted, but it was plain that many girls in the room felt uncomfortable. They felt that they did not live up to the standard, that when they compared themselves to the other girls, they were not good enough, pretty enough, or popular enough. This is the natural outcome of a hyperreal culture that has taught us to constantly compare ourselves with others.

In a hyperreal culture much of our happiness is out of our control because it is tied up in a system of comparison. Advertising is all about social comparison. Advertisers constantly force us to compare our lifestyles and appearances with those of others, with the goal of making us feel dissatisfied with what we already have so that we will let go of our cash. They understand that one of the roles that brands play in our culture is to get us to compare our success in life with that of others. If your coworker with whom you share the same wage buys a better car than you, you will instinctively compare yourself less favorably with that person, asking, "How can he afford such a nice car if he is receiving the same wage as me?" Your happiness is diminished. You go on a diet with a friend who wants to lose the same amount of weight. You keep each other accountable in regard to your eating and you exercise together, but six weeks later you discover that you have lost considerably more weight than your friend. You don't want to admit it, but you secretly feel happy about this outcome. If your friend had lost the same amount of weight, your happiness would not have increased as much.

The philosopher Alain de Botton describes this phenomenon in his excellent book *Status Anxiety*.[6] He makes the point that in societies in which people enjoy large amounts of freedom, that freedom comes at a tremendous price. Because there are no social constraints on their success (unlike during the Middle Ages, when a strict social hierarchy prevented some people from succeeding), people in today's society will constantly compare their well-being with that of those around them. To not succeed in a culture where anyone can succeed deeply affects our self-belief. Thus we find ourselves constantly comparing ourselves to those around us. Instead of happiness, we find anxiety. Even when good things happen to us, they pale in comparison with the shiny, wonderful things offered to us by the hyperreal world. This is because we always compare up not down. The hyperreal offers us unattainable lifestyles, thus inflating our expectations and the reference group with which we compare ourselves. Layard writes:

> If people change their reference group upwards, this can seriously affect their happiness. There are many clear cases where people became objectively better off but felt subjectively worse. One is East Germany, where the living standards of those employed soared after 1990, but their levels of happiness fell; with the reunification of Germany the East Germans began to compare themselves with the West Germans, rather than with the other countries in the former Soviet Bloc.[7]

Comparison anxiety can affect all of us. I have a ministry colleague who was an excellent student in college. After graduation, however, he decided not to enter the corporate world and instead took a job with a mission agency that worked with the poor. He began living on support and committed himself to living simply. He lived in a community house, rode his bicycle often, recycled, bought fair trade, and was deeply aware of the effect that hyperconsumerism was having on our culture. Still, he decided to take a short vacation to visit some of his college friends in Europe, many of whom had well-paying jobs and equally well-heeled lifestyles. The trip went well, and he enjoyed himself, but on return to his normal life, he found himself deeply depressed. For several weeks he could not shake his melancholy or even pinpoint the reason he felt so sad and frustrated. This trip was meant to be a break for him, a reward after years of committed ministry.

My friend came to me, and we discussed what could be going on. I told him that the trip had planted in his mind a what-if scenario. Sure, he was 100 percent committed to his simple lifestyle on intellectual grounds, but seeing the material wealth and lifestyles of his former peers had made him look down on his lifestyle, a lifestyle he was happy with until he compared "up." His situation had not changed; his attitude had.

A crucial thing to understand about happiness is that it is not what we do that has the power to make us happy or unhappy; it is how we view what is happening to us. Often we cannot control what we do and what happens to us, but we can control our expectations. The key to resisting comparison anxiety is to create a value of satisfaction in your life. Most young adults, however, do not have a value of satisfaction; the hyperreal world has not given them healthy expectations of what life can offer.

The problem is that most young adults in the Western world believe the messages of the hyperreal world, and as a result, they are extremely confident about their future. This optimism means that when young adults compare, they compare high. This high level of optimism means that the stakes in the game of comparison are even higher and that the fall will be even greater. For the greater our expectations of life, the more we decrease the likelihood of reaching our goals, and the unhappier we will be as we compare our life to what we thought it would be. The phenomenon of comparison anxiety is made even more acute by the sheer amount of choices available to us in the hyperconsumer world.

CHOICE ANXIETY

Go into any supermarket and try to make a decision over a product that you do not normally buy. Let's say it is laundry detergent. You will first need to navigate your way through the thousands of other products to find the detergent section. Once that task is complete, you are now faced with another problem: how do you choose the right detergent from the multiplicity of options? First, you might look at packaging—which one looks the nicest, which one has the brightest colors, which has the most attractive woman on the container. Feeling superficial for looking too long at the packaging, you decide to buy on price. But what price do you want to spend? Should you go for one of the most expensive brands? Yes, that probably means that it is the best. But hang on—what if your friends see you with the most expensive brand? They will think you are thinking too highly of yourself, blowing your money on the luxury brand. Okay, maybe you should try something cheap. Well, the fact that it is cheap probably means that it won't work well. You begin to look at the mid-range products. Picking up a box of powder, you read the ingredients, which are a bunch of chemicals you have never heard of. Wow! This is really hard. You try to think of what your mother used to use.

Yes, it was that brand. But your neighbor swears by that other brand. After several minutes of exhaustingly weighing the pros and cons of the various choices on offer, you finally take the plunge and pick up a box and head for the checkout. As you drive home, you go over and over in your mind the other choices, feeling anxious as to whether you have made the right choice. This is choice anxiety.

The hyperreal world offers us an overabundance of choices not only in terms of what we buy, but what identity we should hold, how we should live, with whom we should have sex, and with whom we should relate. On one hand it is great to be able to have the freedom to choose, but having to make so many choices so often actually works against happiness. In his book *The Paradox of Choice*, psychologist Barney Schwartz describes how more choices make us less happy:

> As the number of available choices increases, as it has in our consumer culture, the autonomy, control, and liberation this variety brings are powerful and positive. But as the number of choices keeps growing, negative aspects of having a multitude of options begin to appear. As the number of choices grows further, the negatives escalate until we become overloaded. At this point, choice no longer liberates, but debilitates. It might even be said to tyrannize.[8]

Choice anxiety has invaded our love lives—just look at the classic romantic comedy. Almost every movie in this genre is based on a young woman having to choose whom she will love.

Will it be the friendly, reliable, safe but slightly boring guy or the rude, brutish, infuriating yet devilishly handsome bad boy? The heroine finds herself caught in choice anxiety. But this phenomenon is not just for the silver screen; it affects the way many young adults, both single and married, deal with marriage, love, and commitment. Often as I speak with single young adults, I see terror in their eyes as they explain to me that they cannot ever get married because they are afraid they will make the wrong choice and end up stuck in a relationship they cannot get out of. I also speak to young married people who fear that they have made the wrong choice in limiting their options in the face of the sexual smorgasbord the hyperreal world depicts.

Young adults are also now changing jobs at an incredible rate, constantly worrying that they may have made the wrong choice. I have spoken to many young adults who were anxious over what city or what country they should be living in, feeling afraid that they could be missing out on a better life in another geographical location.

Another new form of stress is "party anxiety." Young people text message their friends at other parties to see if their choice of social event for the night is up to the standard of what others are experiencing. Such anxiety can even arise over our religious faith. Many who are raised in faith become anxious over whether they have made the right decision. They constantly look at nonbelievers and evaluate their quality of life. The anxiety of choice means that we are always comparing and often regretting the choices we have made. "A large array of options may diminish the attractiveness of what people actually choose, the reason being that thinking about the attractions of some of the unchosen options detracts from the pleasure derived from the chosen one."[9]

Our lives then become detached from reality; our imaginations play to us constant mind movies of what we could be doing, who we could be with, what we could be enjoying that we never have any realistic chance of achieving. This fantasy mental life becomes the standard against which we measure our lives. Our real lives will always fall short. Yet again we find ourselves being robbed of the chance of happiness by the hyperreal culture as we strive to earn the money to reach a dream world that is never reachable. In the face of all of this pressure, many young adults find themselves experiencing a sped-up version of a midlife crisis that sociologists are labeling the "quarter-life crisis."

QUARTER-LIFE CRISIS

The hyperreal culture tells us that the good life is at our fingertips—all we need is to be wealthy enough to access it. Ironically, our struggle to become wealthy can become one of the main factors in diminishing our happiness. The more we work, the more we become detached from those we love, who in turn provide us with love, intimacy, and acceptance. The promise of work that seemed attractive after high school or college becomes another weight on our shoulders as the burden to earn enough to gain acceptance into the hyperreal world becomes too much. If we are to work this much to get the good stuff, we have to make sacrifices. The young adult years, which we are told are the best times of our life, become harder than we expected as we are called to give up the things that bring us happiness. Kalle Lasn and Bruce Grierson show that it is this sacrifice of relationships for wealth that leads to our diminished happiness, which then causes us to desire more products and to work more and become detached from the things that give us happiness. "Our quest for money widens the gulf between ourselves and our family/community. Our growing alienation then creates an inner sense of social and spiritual emptiness. That's when advertisers get into the loop by assuring us that their products can make us whole again. We go out and buy their products, which requires money. And so we're back at the beginning, the quest for money."[10]

The pressure of this treadmill proves too much for many. Young adults find themselves stuck in life, asking, "How do I find my way out? How do I find happiness in a culture that has a vested interest in keeping me unhappy? How do I find identity in a culture that sees only the surface? How do I make the right choices in a culture of so much variety?"

For many middle-class young adults, their early twenties are a time of great promise and excitement. Our culture worships youth, so these twentysomethings are still young enough to be hip yet old enough to have power to influence their lives. All kinds of social, sexual, and romantic possibilities lie ahead; the job market is slanted in their favor; and their high levels of disposable income mean that they have a world of entertainment and travel opportunities ahead of them. Many young women particularly feel this pressure as they are expected to have an exciting career and a fantastic social life; be in a relationship; travel when possible; have children at some point; appear attractive, fit, and fashionable; and have enough disposable income to live well. To achieve all of these things is almost impossible. Yet we are told that it is possible. We hear the pop culture mantras of our day: "Believe in yourself." "Reach for the stars." "Follow your dreams." These mantras sound as if they would be good ideas to apply to our lives, but they simply do not cut it in the real world, as Jean Twenge makes clear:

> "Following your dreams" sounds like a good principle, until you realize that every waiter in L.A. is following his or her dreams of becoming an actor, and most of them won't succeed. Most people are not going to realize their dreams, because most people do not dream of becoming accountants, social workers, or trash collectors—just to name three jobs that society can't do without but nevertheless factor into few childhood fantasies.[11]

As we begin to reach our quarter-life, the reality that life is not as rosy as our culture tells us begins to emerge. We find that our childhood dreams are not realized. Or when we do achieve a dream, such as visiting the Egyptian pyramids or moving into a certain hip neighborhood, we discover that a whole bunch of people just like us have achieved the same thing; and so now that we have achieved it, we do not really feel satisfied. Thus many young adults reach their thirtieth birthday and experience a kind of crisis, as Twenge goes on to explain: "Because we expect to marry and have children later, it's more acceptable to spend your entire twenties pursuing 'dream' careers . . . Many twentysomethings struggle with the decision to keep pursuing their dream, or cut their losses and go home. More and more young people are going to find themselves at thirty without a viable career, house, or any semblance of stability."[12]

Sadly, there is no way out of this crisis; and many will enter depression while others will simply assume that they are in this boat not because our culture of hyperconsumerism has set them up to fail, but because they must have been doing something wrong.[13] They then may leave their partner, have an affair, change jobs, move to the beach, get a tattoo and new rebel attitude, or renovate their house. My friend Dayan Ramalingam noted that today people tend to have affairs because they have had a change in worldview rather than because they just can no longer hold back their lust for the plumber. They have discovered that life is not what they expected; thus their leaving their spouse or engaging in an extramarital relationship is more about trying to find happiness and allay a loss of meaning.

The consequences of many quarter-life crises can affect young people for the rest of their lives, as Alexandra Robbins and Abby Wilner make clear: "At the fragile, doubt-ridden age during which the quarterlife crisis occurs, the ramifications can be extremely dangerous."[14] Very often when the inevitable failure of consumerism occurs, the worldview that gets thrown out the door is the Christian worldview; and many attempt to arrive at happiness by ferociously pursuing consumerism without any Christian ethic of restraint.

SEVEN

The Rub Between
Real Life and Hyperreality

REAL LIFE

The problem with the hyperreal world is that we don't live there; we live in the world of reality. It is not a world in which we can live, because it does not really exist. It is disconnected from the realm of human experience. We wish our lives were as exciting and glamorous as the kind of lives promised to us by the hyperreal world, but we are wedded to the world of reality; we live in the ordinary. Intrinsically we know this—we know we are trapped in the world of the mundane, the ordinary. We see the hyperreal world as something that can save us from the boredom of everyday existence. If we can just buy that product, get that luxury car, find a better relationship, improve our sex lives, lose that weight, go on that overseas trip—then we will escape reality, enter into the hyperreal world, and find meaning. In fact, one of the key messages of the hyperreal world is that if we are experiencing anything less than a super-star life, we must have little or no meaning in our lives.

Often we get fooled because we know that hyperreality

cannot deliver us the perfect life. We know that our lives are wedded to reality, but occasionally there is an overlap between reality and hyperreality. It could be an overseas vacation where everything is exciting and glamorous; it could be that high you get as you make a big purchase; it could be the exhilaration you feel as you move into your new apartment. For a brief moment the two spheres cross; hyperreality breaks into your mundane, everyday life, but we all know that this is fleeting—the vacation must end, the purchase will become passé, the new apartment will lose its novelty. We will always return to reality.

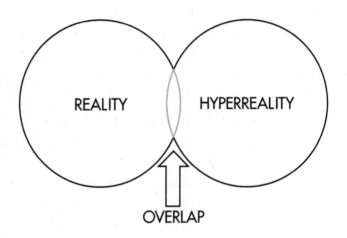

Often, young adults will come to me to talk about how unhappy and frustrated they are with their lives. As I help them dig deeper into their situation, we discover that they are struggling with many of the issues that are simply part of life—responsibility, pain, the mundane nature of everyday life, the fact that they are getting older. Nevertheless, they think these issues are abnormal and no one else is struggling with them. I remember one young woman in one of my teaching sessions who shared with the group that she had broken down while sitting at her computer after the pressure of trying to "keep up appearances" on her social networking Web site proved too much. She said it seemed that from looking at all of her friends' social networking Web pages, they all were having great lives and wonderful times, and her life was mundane in comparison. She had found herself playing down the "ordinary" elements of her life online to make herself more impressive. In the end she decided to commit social networking Web site suicide and shut down her account, thus freeing herself from the addiction of having to compete. Her courage in sharing led many of the other young adults in the room to share similar frustrations and pressures. I thought to myself, *If only young people could understand the true nature of life.*

In many ways the real world is the flip side of hyperreality. It is the same world in which people have lived throughout the course of human history. I think that we know that deep down, but we prefer to live under the illusion that the hyperreal dream is just around the corner for us. The mundane nature of our real lives simply seems to make the glamour of the hyperreal world all the more appealing.

MUNDANE

With fast-paced music videos, action-packed video games, and a vast array of other forms of entertainment on offer to youth in the West, young people at the beginning of the twenty-first century are accustomed to being constantly entertained. The hyperreal culture promises us a life of constant interest and excitement. I always laugh at the way computers are portrayed on TV and in the movies. The detective is always able to pull up a file in seconds, to access information on the criminals he is tracking in the blink of an eye. I contrast this to my reality of dealing with my PC. Often I go and make a cup of coffee because I have to wait several minutes while my PC turns itself on, loads up, and runs through its virus check routine. Life is not edited like movies are. In reality we have to face the mundane nature of life: we have to wash the dishes, pay the bills, and rest our bodies to survive.

It is fascinating to see how people in the remaining two-thirds of the world do not have the expectation to be entertained all the time. On a trip to the South Pacific, I saw a Polynesian man sitting cross-legged in his backyard staring at the ground. Several hours later I again drove past the same man, and he had not moved. He did not seem upset or frustrated; he was happy simply to relax by sitting in his backyard, not doing anything in particular. Such a view of life is hard to fathom for us living in the shadow of the hyperreal world. When we do encounter the inevitable periods of the mundane in life, we become bored and see this as evidence of the poor nature of our lives. We say to ourselves that if our lives really meant something, we would not be bored; we would be doing something interesting all the time. One thing that frustrates us, however, is the reality that we cannot be doing exciting things all the time, because we must work.

TOIL AND WORK

In the hyperreal world we constantly see people who find meaning in their work. The people we see on TV and in movies have jobs that are exciting and glamorous, that take them all over the world, that help them meet celebrities and interesting people. The reality for most of us, however, is that we will not find work that enlivens us. Even those people who enjoy their jobs, who do find meaning in their work, will have periods when they are bored or frustrated. But for many of us—most likely, the majority—we will not find fulfillment in our work; it will be something we do to pay the bills. I constantly meet young adults who worked hard in high school to get into certain universities in order to get into particular careers. They persevered at the university and finally got a job in the field they had been working toward, only to find that the job was nothing like they expected. So they left in frustration at wasting so much of their time and effort.

Toil is part of life: we must exercise to keep our bodies healthy, we must weed our gardens to make them productive, we must practice personal hygiene to avoid becoming infected, we must work to support ourselves, and we must cook meals in order to eat. This fact is lost on us, though, when we look at the hyperreal world. Instead of seeing work as part of the mundane nature of human existence, we see it as another indicator that our lives are heading in a wrong direction. For the exciting lives we see on television, in advertising, and in the movies seem to magnificently avoid toil, responsibility, and consequences.

CONSEQUENCES

The movie hero fights off three attackers. Again and again he is hit in the head. Blood runs down his face. Having beaten off the villains, he continues on in his adventures with no sign of concussion, internal bleeding, or permanent damage. Later in the film, our hero and a woman he has just met have passionate (and we presume unprotected) sex in an office. Of course she does not get pregnant, and neither of them contracts a sexually transmitted disease. And of course no one gets overly emotionally attached. At the climax of the film, our hero chases the arch-villain across the city, smashing countless cars. Finally, he catches up with and kills the villain. Of course the police do not charge him with dangerous driving. No one is charged with murder, and there is no investigation. In the hyperreal world, people rarely suffer consequences for their actions.

In the real world, however, there is always a consequence. If we make an impulse purchase with our credit card, we have to pay the bill at the end of the month. If we eat only junk food, our health will be badly affected. If we drive too fast, we can kill others. Our disposable lifestyles in the West have a direct consequence on the environment. If we treat people poorly, we can upset others' lives. Life in reality is filled with consequences to our actions; we are not disconnected individuals as the hyper-real world portrays. Rather, we live in a connected world where the decisions we make affect our environment and those around us, whether in our neighborhood or on the other side of the world.

INJUSTICE

Right after high school, I spent some time observing and working in a poor area of Los Angeles. The street I stayed on was about the length of an average suburban street, yet it was home to thousands of disadvantaged Latino and Cambodian people. I was shocked by the poverty in the area. The street was the crossroad between fierce gang territories and had seen its fair share of violence. At night I would go to sleep to the sounds of gunshots. This was the worst place I had ever been. I had never experienced such need and had never felt in so much danger.

I spent one evening having dinner with a Cambodian family who had escaped to America during Pol Pot's genocidal regime. As I sat in their cramped second-floor, two-room apartment, I could see the crack dealers operating in the alley. Caucasian middle-class people were driving up in brand-new cars to purchase their daily crack cocaine. The family offered me a simple Cambodian dish, and we sat down to eat together. Still in shock from the poverty of the area, I asked the father of the family how they felt about their neighborhood. The father replied that he was truly grateful to God for giving them such a wonderful place to live while their relatives back in Cambodia suffered so much. My hell was their heaven.

When I began writing this book, I wanted to write about the effects of hyperconsumerism on our personal faith and happiness. I have many friends and colleagues who speak far more articulately than I do of the effects of our rampant consumerism on the poor of our planet. Furthermore, there are many outstanding books, both Christian and secular, that address this issue with far more depth and expertise than I can here. But I could not write on this topic without mentioning just a few small but shocking realities about the way hyperconsumer culture makes us act in the face of so much suffering.

The hyperreal world says to us very little if anything about the terrible plight of most people on this planet. Behind the deafening sounds of the hyperreal message are the quiet voices of millions upon millions of poor and disenfranchised people whose idea of heaven looks something like our standard of living. The attacks on September 11, 2001, in Manhattan killed around three thousand people, but experts estimate that ten times that number of children are dying every day as a result of poverty. The World Bank states that in 2001, about 1.1 billion humans worldwide lived off less than one U.S. dollar per day. Preventable and treatable diseases, such as AIDS, malaria, and tuberculosis, kill fifteen thousand Africans daily. All over the Two-Thirds World, old people, families, young adults, and children live in abject poverty and suffer and die as a result of poor sanitation, disease, extreme poverty, war, forced prostitution, and slavery. Yet in the comfortable West, with its unbelievable standards of prosperity, many young adults feel that they are not doing well because they cannot regularly travel or buy the latest clothes or gadgets. You can spend all day wishing you had the lifestyle of a Hollywood celebrity, but the fact of the matter is that if you are born in the West, you have won the cosmic lottery.

It is not just us rich in the West who become trapped in the game of comparison. The proliferation of global media means that even those who cannot afford the hyperreal dream are nonetheless still exposed to the alluring messages of hyper-consumerism, as Ash Barker, who lives in a slum with the poor, passionately communicates:

> Those in the slums are watching the same—if not more—dramas and advertisements, which depict what life is supposed to be like in mansions. As a result of the media nurturing the same wants and aspirations as the rich, a large proportion of urban dwellers, not having the wherewithal to fulfill them, experience a toxic cocktail of guilt (in not living the way they and their children are "supposed" to live) and resentment (of those who can afford to live like that). These emotions of guilt and resentment in urban life have already found some expression through violence and terrorism. Our ability to reach those who are caught in the grip of urban poverty will determine the stability of the world's population this century. This situation facing humanity has never been so extreme.[1]

The hyperreal has no answers for this situation. If the whole world began to consume in the same way we do in the developed world, we would be in serious trouble. We need a new vision of life, not just for our own sense of personal fulfillment and happiness but to rearrange the order of the world. It is vital for us as Christians to ask, "What is our responsibility in the face of such extreme discrepancies in lifestyle?"

PAIN

When I am asked, "How can I escape the hold that the hyper-consumer world has on my life? What can I do?" I often issue people a challenge. I tell them to spend the next weekend at home. I tell them to stay in; to turn off the TV, phones, and computer; and not to contact their friends. I say to put away magazines and books, hide the iPod, and switch off the radio for the entire weekend. Most people find this challenge too hard, but a few have actually tried with stunning results. Most initially enjoy the space, but then after a few hours, boredom sets in and many will sleep. Come Saturday night most find themselves breaking down. One guy who got back to me after trying the challenge found himself, after twenty-four hours of no stimulation or distraction, sitting on his bed sobbing. In the quiet all kinds of pain from people's pasts emerge, and doubts about their worth invade the minds of otherwise confident people. Some find themselves almost paranoid, wondering what their friends are doing and whether they are having fun without them. This exercise illustrates the way in which the hyperconsumer culture acts as a smoke screen, distracting us from the causes of our unhappiness, as Henri Nouwen affirms in his book *Reaching Out*:

> It is the most basic human loneliness that threatens us and is so hard to face. Too often we will do everything possible to avoid the confrontation with the experience of being alone, and sometimes we are able to create the most ingenious devices to prevent ourselves from being reminded of this condition. Our culture has become most sophisticated in the avoidance of pain, not only our physical pain but our emotional and mental pain as well. . . . When we have no project to finish, no friend to visit, no book to read, no television to watch . . . and when we are left all alone by ourselves, we are brought so close to the revelation of our basic human aloneness and so afraid of experiencing an all-pervasive sense of loneliness that we will do anything to get busy again and continue the game which makes us believe that everything is fine after all.[2]

The exercise in a sense allows us to see what it is to live life without any of the messages that consumer culture gives us regarding our own identity. Willow Creek pastor Bill Hybels, when trying to encourage Christians to live more faithful lives, asked, "Who are we when no one is looking?" Maybe the question we need to ask ourselves now is, "Who are we when we are not buying, owning, or experiencing?" Many find that once the feedback loops of identity that hyperconsumer culture gives us are shut off, we discover that we do not know who we are. "The consuming self, unmasked, reveals a terrible absence. There is no substance to our being, nothing there but the appearances, the 'outside,' the 'looking good,' which has become, as the ad says, 'everything.' There is a hole underneath it all. It is a discovery frighteningly made in those moments of true solitude when we are no longer producing, consuming, marketing, or buying."[3]

We find that behind the buzz of contemporary life we are in pain. For many of us this is a frightening realization, because the hyperreal world has no answer for our pain. In any TV sitcom, characters may face problems, but almost always those problems are resolved by the end of the episode. You will never see in a sitcom a female character who struggles to allow herself to be loved because she was sexually abused as a child. You will never discover that the funny guy character actually is bipolar or see a character struggle with alcohol dependency issues. In many ways the hyperreal world has fooled us into believing that at best pain is not a part of life or at worst that pain can be avoided. The vast majority of us, however, will find our lives touched by pain in some way.

We are broken people. For some, that brokenness will touch us only for a while; for others, pain will last a lifetime. In a world in which divorce, illness, sexual abuse, depression, stress, financial problems, relationship issues, family breakdown, codependency, addiction, disease, crime, disability, and betrayal exist as part of the everyday fabric of life, there is little chance of living a life that is not touched in some sense by these issues.

INSIGNIFICANCE IN AN AGE OF CELEBRITY

The hyperreal world tells us that by making the right consumer choices, by becoming popular and creating an exciting portfolio of experiences, we can gain significance. In the hyperreal world, there is no greater significance than celebrity. Increasingly in the field of politics and even social change, celebrities are used to influence public opinion. But as you take apart the idea of celebrity and ask why it is appealing to so many, celebrity holds the myth that to be famous is to be noticed, to be recognized. It is a chance to be loved. The rest of those in our society who never become famous, however, face lives of insignificance. Our funerals will not be attended by thousands of mourning people. Yes, we have a chance to touch those around us—our family and friends and those with whom we work—but most will never see the desire to make a significant impact in our world fulfilled. Instead, after we pass, our lives will simply fade back into the fabric of human history, unrecorded except in family photo albums and our friends' and family's memories. For it is death more than anything else that pulls down the paper tiger that is hyperreality.

DEATH

For all of the hyperreal world's obsession with youthfulness, we exist in a world in which people age. It is simply one of the realities of life that as each moment passes by, we age and our bodies break down and decay. Nevertheless, our culture hides from this fact. We like our elderly virile and active, such as the people we see in retirement fund advertising, sailing a yacht with beaming smiles or starting a postretirement e-commerce Web site. Our society is youth focused. We do not like to see our elderly frail, weak, and pale, for they then become gasping, hobbling advertisements for death, reminding us that one day we will be in their place. While other cultures celebrate the elderly for their experience and wisdom, our culture provides plastic surgery for those who wish to look young. We sell wrinkle-reducing cream and mugs for forty-year-olds emblazoned with crude jibes, such as "Over the Hill"; models get younger and younger; video game consoles are marketed to thirtysomethings; marriage is feared by the young; and fifty-year-old executives are abandoned as obsolete. We attempt to skip the death question by fixating our gaze on the ideal of youth—the beginnings of life. Even so, the laws of physics are set in concrete for all of our efforts. We cannot turn back time.

As a culture we shun the notion of death. We flee from it the way our great-grandparents blushed at the mention of sex. We justifiably speak today of past eras as times of repressed sexuality, but we fail to remember that people then were much more open about death than we are. Maybe our great-grandchildren will label us death-repressed. It seems that most people whose hope is in the hyperreal world can't wait to get away from the funeral service and move on to the wake and forget the whole experience, instead speaking about football over a beer at an appropriately quiet volume. Paradoxically, we cannot get past the fact that we are unable to totally repress our feelings about death.

The flip side to the past era's prudish views toward sex was a hidden fascination with the act of making love. Men would go to bars where women would daringly expose their ankles. The saloons of the American frontier or the Moulin Rouge of Paris was where you found the underside of Victorian era sexuality. But where do we find the underside of our contemporary uneasiness with death? We find the underside in the broad spectrum of youth subcultures that move from goth to emo to metal, which hold suffering and death as a countercultural badge from which to critique mainstream society and the myth of hyperreal culture.

With the exception of the loved one or acquaintance who dies, our contemporary notion of death is delivered via the television screen, be it through the innocent victim of a drunk driver staring out of her best photo carefully selected by a grieving father, the celebrity who overdoses in a storm of hidden loneliness, or the casualty who has been reduced to a mere "number of killed" in a war in a faraway country. We have become distanced from death. The cinema has become the place where we can access this unspoken part of human existence in the dark without interacting with those around us.

Perhaps our misgivings with death come from the idea that nothing follows death. For, as my tenth-grade history teacher stressed, "We are nothing more than cosmic accidents. There is no God or heaven or spiritual realm. Get over it now, kids; it's a fairy tale." This view of hard scientific rationalism has struggled to survive in the face of a resurgent spirituality, but its talons are strong, and they dig deepest in the face of the ever-present reality of death. Our cultural rush to lose ourselves in pleasure, to experience, to buy more stuff, to keep traveling is fueled by our unspoken and unrealized fear of death. Paradoxically then, we are in denial of death, yet we are a culture at the mercy of death. It holds us in its unrelenting grip; we feel its hot, sticky breath on the back of our necks. It is indomitable. We find it in the violence that haunts our culture's homes; we find it in the injustice of global poverty and starvation; and we sense it in war and crime, in the destruction of the environment, in disease and sickness, and in the hardness of the human heart.

I remember visiting a relative who had been rushed to the hospital on a Friday night. As I went to the restroom, I passed a ward where I was confronted with the image of an elderly woman, alone, gaunt, and ravaged by disease. Her room overlooked a panoramic view of the skyscrapers of downtown. I knew that behind the twinkling lights of the city, there were young adults dancing, scoring, partying, spending, and shopping. Yet here was this dying woman, alone with only her fading mortality as companion. This was the future of most of the young adults out on the town in the distance. This is our future. One day many of us are going to fight the specter of life-threatening disease. Some of us will hold our loved ones as they say good-bye and die in our arms; some of us will deal with the horrible effects of aging, of our bodies and minds coming to their end. And all of us, every single one of us, will one day have to face death.

Many of you as you read will recoil from what I am writing,

finding it simply too hard to face, but how we integrate our eventual deaths into our lives now is crucial to the sort of lives we lead. A friend once told me that we should not make any major decisions in life without walking around a graveyard, for death is the ultimate lens with which to view our life projects. When it comes to death, our neon-light, hard-rock culture falls silent. Nothing in the hyperreal culture can save us from aging and death. Theologian Gordon Wenham wrote, "Consumerism focuses entirely on this world and its pleasures, so that death itself is the ultimate disproof of all that consumers hold dear. It may be for this reason that in our era death is the great taboo topic that people rarely talk about. When it happens to someone near them, they try to pretend it has not happened."[4]

Our fear of death is rooted in our cultural rejection of God. As a culture we have chased after the supposed freedom that life without God brings, yet we pay a massive price for this freedom—constant fear of death. Jürgen Moltmann is right to observe that this rejection of God ultimately perverts our humanity:

In our modern society human beings have apparently been turned into voracious monsters. They are tormented by an unquenchable thirst for life. . . . The more they have, the more they want, so their appetite is endless and can never be appeased. Why have people in our modern world become so perverted? Because both consciously and unconsciously they are dominated by the fear of death. Their greed for life is really their fear of death; and the fear of death finds expression in an unbridled hunger for power. "You only live once!" we are told. "You might miss out on something!" This hunger for pleasure, for possessions, for power; the thirst for recognition through success and admiration—that is the perversion of modern men and women. That is their godlessness. The person who loses God makes a god out of himself. And in this way a human being becomes a proud and unhappy mini-god.[5]

This is the place we find ourselves—unhappy mini-gods. This is even true of many of us who are of faith. Our Savior has been dethroned, and we sit awkwardly on the thrones of our lives, miserable and frustrated. Hyperreality has made our faith impotent.

EIGHT

How Hyperreality
Ruins Faith

When I speak to groups about hyperreality, I notice that people are initially quite energized. As we begin to take apart hyperreality, people enjoy talking about things that have great bearing on their daily lives—things they may never have thought of, let alone discussed. People get a kick out of finding the different means advertisers use to get them to buy what they don't need. But as we begin to move the discussion away from hyperreality to the reality of our lives, people often feel strangely comforted. They feel that it is okay to sometimes feel bored, that they are not the only ones who struggle with pain, and that many others in the room also struggle. Often people will become moved and share with others in the group, relieved that they do not have to live up to the high expectations that hyperreal culture places on their lives.

Then, after the section of the teaching that focuses on the reality of our lives, a strange mood often comes over the participants, a kind of flatness. For some time I could not understand why. But then in a discussion with a friend who is an active member of Alcoholics Anonymous, a coin dropped for me. My friend explained that when he stopped drinking, his health, well-being, and overall life improved dramatically. To his surprise, despite his life improving, he began to become depressed. Not understanding why, he took his problem to his sponsor. He discovered that many addicts struggle with grief after they quit their habit. Sure, their lives are better, but they had to say good-bye to something that has been a large part of their lives. They are grieving a false hope, but a hope nonetheless.

It is the same with hyperreality. We can expose it, see the lies and myths behind it, and see the way it ruins our happiness, but some part of us will miss it. For many of us, hyperreality has been our hope since we were children. Some people have come to my talks on hyperreality and left determined to rid their lives of the influence of hyperreality. Some have written to me a year later saying that they could not live without the hope of hyperreality in their lives and have decided to go for the dream of hyperreality even though they know it is a fallacy.

Others attend my speaking engagements and try to expunge their lives of any shred of consumerism. They will try to become ethical consumers, which is something I believe is vital. The selling of products that harm and enslave others through unfair labor practices and that damage the creation for which we are responsible should be on every Christian's moral radar. However, if we only change what we buy, I believe that we will change very little. We can buy fair trade and organic yet still live under the framework of consumerism, running from commitment and community, living for self, chasing experience at the expense of intimacy and connection, and treating others like objects. The answer to our dilemma is to be found in faith, worship, and adherence.

Once while walking through a mall, I heard my name called, and I turned and recognized a young woman who had attended some of my training sessions. She sheepishly apologized that she worked in a retail store that sold jewelry to teenage girls. I laughed and told her not to feel guilty. If we only affect surface change and do not address the soul issues that cause us to live under the framework of hyperconsumerism, we will simply become brown-rice Pharisees, looking down our noses at those who cannot afford to shop at the organic market. To be truly free of the lure of the hyperreal world, we need to examine the way the hyperreal world diminishes our faith.

CONTROL

As I am writing this, several young women have run past my office window, each resplendent in her stylish warm-up suit, must-have attire for jogging, and each wearing the obligatory white earphones attached to her MP3 player, identifying her as part of a tribe. I wonder why they are running; maybe it is to be healthy, and that would be a good thing. But I know this culture too well and suspect that part of their motivation to run is to gain control over their lives. Maybe they want a better body to control their boyfriends' feelings toward them. Maybe they want to look better than the other girls in the office so as to control their place in the office female hierarchy. Maybe they feel that they can control the effects of aging by staying fit, telling themselves that they cannot control their chronological age but they can control their biological age. Sadly, our culture exploits our anxieties about being loved, about being accepted. It exploits the fact that we cannot control time or death or aging or car accidents or cancer or tsunamis or terrorists. We are not God.

The book of Genesis records a fascinating encounter between Adam and Eve and the serpent. Adam and Eve live in the environment created by God especially for their needs. They have everything they could possibly want; they are in wonderful relationship with each other, with the environment, and with God. They want for nothing; all they have to do is obey God's commandment not to eat from the Tree of the Knowledge of Good and Evil.

Into the picture comes the serpent, with a dangerous question. He asks Eve why God has told them not to eat of the Tree of the Knowledge of Good and Evil. Eve responds that God has told them not to eat from that tree because it will cause death. The serpent realizes their weakness and replies that what God has said is not true. They will not die. In fact, they will have their eyes opened, and they will become just like God. The serpent is offering them the power to control their world, to move from being dependents who live in harmony with God and have everything provided for them, to reject God as provider.

Adam and Eve's anxiety causes them to reject a caring, trusting relationship with God and to pursue their own individual control of their world. Nevertheless, they are not God. They can attempt to act like God, but they do not have the attributes of God, the power and ability of God to control. So they trade in their wonderful environment, their eternal life, their relationship with God, their relationship with each other, and their relationship with nature for a cheap imitation of control. The result of their rebellion is that humans walk in the shadow of death, of time, of suffering, of environmental degradation, of relational conflict, and of separation from God.

In this story we are all Adam and Eve, and the serpent questions us. A Jewish story told by the rabbis explains our position:

> Zuzya once asked his brother, wise Rabbi Elimelekh: "Dear brother, in the Scriptures we read that the souls of all men were comprised in Adam. So we too must have been present when he ate the apple. I do not understand how I could have let him eat it! And how could you have let him eat it?" Elimelekh replied: "We had to just as all had to. For had he not eaten, the poison of the snake would have remained within him for all eternity. He would have thought, 'All I need do is eat of this tree, and I shall be as God—all I need do is eat of this tree, and I shall be as God.'"[1]

As the rabbis' story explains, the serpent's question still reverberates around our heads and hearts every day. We hear it in advertisements, in TV shows, in the questions and recommendations of our friends, family, and fellow workers. We are told, "Grab control yourself—it's the only way!" Sadly, in an attempt to escape anxiety, we walk away from God, the only real cure to our worry. Walter Brueggemann explains:

It is only God . . . who can deal with the anxiety among us . . . The causes for anxiety among us are wrongly discerned . . . Our mistake is to pursue autonomous freedom. Freedom which does not discern the boundaries of human life leaves us anxious. The attempts to resolve anxiety in our culture are largely psychological, economic, cosmetic. They are bound to fail because they do not approach the causes. Our public life is largely premised on an exploitation of our common anxiety. The advertising of consumerism and the drives of the acquisitive society, like the serpent, seduce [people] into believing there are securities apart from the reality of God.[2]

So our life is spent walking through a world of things that offer us "securities apart from the reality of God." And let's face it—some of those securities look pretty good. But like paintings by Monet, they look great from a distance; get up close and they are a mess. Unfortunately, most of us sign up on the forty-eight-month direct debit plan before we can get up close to see what a bad deal we have entered into. We lurch forward to grab control, to get as much freedom as we can, to keep our options open. Then—*crack!*—the trap snaps tight over our hand. Welcome to slavery!

COMFORTABLE SLAVES

Thinking of yourself as a slave is probably difficult. When I think of slaves, I think of the Africans ripped from their homeland and taken to the New World; I think of the Israelites toiling to serve their Egyptian overlords; and I also think of many today who live in the Two-Thirds World and are paid miniscule sums to make consumer items that we take for granted. The slavery I am talking about is very different from these kinds of very real and tragic forms of slavery: I am talking about being a slave to self. This is a form of slavery that trades in meaning, community, identity, and relationship for the myths of freedom, choice, and control.

Nikolai Berdyaev was drawn to Christianity after living his life under oppressive Soviet rule. He noticed that even though his friends, family, and fellow citizens desperately wanted freedom from their cruel rulers, bizarrely there was a part of them that enjoyed the comfort of being slaves. He wrote, "Man seeks freedom. There is within him an immense drive towards freedom, and yet not only does he easily fall into slavery, but he even loves slavery."[3]

The Israelites had a similar story. God led them into freedom, yet as soon as the going got hard, they started to reminisce about their days of slavery. In a way we can identify with them. In slavery they had no freedom, but they had a bed to sleep on and knew where their next meal was coming from. Likewise in the shiny culture of the West in which we live, we secretly enjoy our slavery; we know the ground rules, and we know how to play the game. Sure, we want freedom from the oppression of always having to measure up, to live life as a brand, constantly feeling the pressure to be interesting, attractive, and cool. But we cannot imagine what life would be like if we left all of that pressure behind. So we attempt to live half slave and half free.

We have designed ingenious ways to make half-serious attempts at true freedom. We are like an inmate who makes a dash for the perimeter wall of the prison. We hoist ourselves up, look over at the vast free fields outside, get scared, and slip back down into the prison, energized by our glimpse of what freedom looks like but still wholeheartedly in jail. The most powerful forms of slavery do not just restrain us physically; they capture our dreams, holding our imaginations captive. When you have captured someone's imagination, you don't need to physically restrain your prisoner, for he knows nothing but restraint. The captive operates as almost a half person—defeated and broken down in mind, body, and spirit. This is where many of us are, for most of us cannot even begin to dream of another world, another culture that does not look like the hyperreal world. Could we dare to dream that there is not only another way to live, but that this other way to live is actually superior to the way of life that we are living now—a way of life that could exceed our greatest expectations?

IDOLS

It is hard to dream of another reality when we are caught in the prison of idol worship. The hyperreal world is fresh and new, but really it is just the latest incarnation of one of humanity's greatest reoccurring faults, our habit of worshiping that which is created. Throughout the Bible we find the people of God faced with a polar choice, to trust in God and his provision and care or to create images and illusions to worship. Because we have free choice, we are able to choose whom or what we will worship. As the great Jewish rabbi Abraham Heschel taught, "Every one of us is bound to have an ultimate object of worship, yet he is free to choose the object of his worship. He cannot live without it; it may be either a fictitious or a real object, God or an idol."[4] It is this choice that is at the heart of biblical faith.

The primary confession of Israel, the people of God, begins with the Shema. The Shema is both a prayer and a confession and is considered by Jews as the most important Jewish prayer. Religious Jews say it in both the morning and evening. The Shema comes from Deuteronomy 6:

> Hear, O Israel: The LORD our God, the LORD is one. Love the LORD your God with all your heart and with all your soul and with all your strength. These commandments that I give you today are to be upon your hearts. Impress them on your children. Talk about them when you sit at home and when you walk along the road, when you lie down and when you get up. Tie them as symbols on your hands and bind them on your foreheads. Write them on the doorframes of your houses and on your gates (vv. 4–9).

This verse was a clear statement that, unlike the surrounding nations, the people of God were defined by their belief in one God. This was not just an abstract statement about belief in God. By stating that God was one, a person was declaring that God, therefore, was the ultimate authority over the whole of life. The Shema is not just a statement of belief but also a prayer of submission. This had huge implications for the lifestyle of the believer, as my friend and mentor Alan Hirsch writes in his wonderful book, *The Forgotten Ways*:

> What this meant to the person(s) coming under this claim is that no longer could there be different gods for the different spheres of life, a god of the temple, another god of politics, a different god for fertility in the field, and yet another for the river, etc. Rather, Yahweh is the ONE God who rules over every aspect of life and the world. Yahweh is the Lord of home, field, politics, work, etc., and the religious task was to honor this ONE God in and through all the aspects of life.[5]

When the writers of the New Testament addressed Jesus as Lord, all of the meaning of the Shema was behind the statement. Jesus is Yahweh, and we are called to bring the whole of our lives under this calling. This, however, is where the insidious nature of idols enters the equation. By worshiping idols, we give ourselves a "way out" of God being the authority over the whole of our lives. By worshiping idols, we try to wrestle some of the control back from God; we try to play the spiritual game without God. Eugene Peterson notes that idols are kinds of non-gods that are often much easier to stomach than Yahweh.

Idols are non-gods and as such are much more congenial to us than God, for we not only have the pleasure of making them, using our wonderful imaginations and skills in creative ways, but also of controlling them. They are gods with all of the God taken out so that we can continue to be our own gods. There are innumerable ways in which we can make idols for ourselves . . . It is no wonder that idol-making and idol-worshipping have always been the most popular religious game in town.[6]

Peterson makes a crucial point: the worship of idols is ultimately about the worship of ourselves. In many ways the hyper-real culture we live in is not an idol in itself; rather, it is a delivery system that serves up to us daily the idols of our choice and the addictions of our particular weaknesses. It could be overeating, dangerous undereating, social competition, or an obsession with wealth, materialism, selfishness, or sexuality detached from relationship. Whatever our weak spots, the hyperreal culture will put it before our faces and offer us the opportunity to turn it into idol worship. For the follower of Christ, this is serious stuff; we are faced with the reality that our faith may have been compromised.

The worship of idols and the self carries serious ramifications. God's positive agenda for our lives, as agents that reflect his glory on earth, is given over to the self-destructive nature. Paul's description of humanity in his letter to the Romans is relevant to us and our false hopes in the hyperreal world: "For although they knew God, they neither glorified him as God nor gave thanks to him, but their thinking became futile and their foolish hearts were darkened. Although they claimed to be wise, they became fools and exchanged the glory of the immortal God for images made to look like mortal man and birds and animals and reptiles" (1:21–23).

By choosing to worship things made of stone and wood—mere objects—idol worshipers make a devastating error. We objectify the whole of life when we worship idols that are simply objects. If our culture holds materialism as one of its highest values, the converse reality is that the spiritual, the sacred, and all sense of mystery will be sucked out of life. We will then turn the people we love into objects, mere things, whose only purpose is to deliver us happiness and pleasure; we rob them of their humanity. When we objectify life we rob sexuality of all of its romance and relationship; sex becomes technique, an act of masturbation at which another person just happens to be present. In a culture where we have become mere things, courtship is robbed of its seduction, intimacy, and delightful playfulness. Instead, we are left with the cold mechanical nature of speed dating, which looks more like a factory production line than true human-to-human interaction. In a world of objects, communities become zip codes, homes become houses. The victims of war and starvation become meaningless statistics scrolling across the bottom of our TV screens as we watch the morning news. At this point we begin to lose our humanity; we move toward the robotic, robbed of our God-given freedom. For as John Kavanaugh perceptively warns, "Having patterned ourselves after the image of our commodities, we become disenfranchised of our very humanness. Reduced to commodities, we lose the intimacy of personal touch. We cannot truly see or listen as vibrant men and women . . . We do not walk in freedom, since we are paralyzed by what is. Such is the result of idolatry. Those who make idols and put their trust in them become like them."[7]

We then understand what the words of Psalm 115 mean in our time in history. The warning of the psalmist is just as relevant to us today as it was when it was written.

> Why do the nations say,
>   "Where is their God?"
> Our God is in heaven;
>   he does whatever pleases him.
> But their idols are silver and gold,
>   made by the hands of men.
> They have mouths, but cannot speak,
>   eyes, but they cannot see;
> they have ears, but cannot hear,
>   noses, but they cannot smell;
> they have hands, but cannot feel,
>   feet, but they cannot walk;
>   nor can they utter a sound with their throats.
> Those who make them will be like them,
>   and so will all who trust in them (vv. 2–8).

If we continue reading from Paul's comments regarding idol worship in Romans 1, we find other points worth noting. Paul said that after people had exchanged the glory of God for the worship of man-made things, "God gave them over in the sinful desires of their hearts to sexual impurity for the degrading of their bodies with one another. They exchanged the truth of God for a lie, and worshiped and served created things rather than the Creator—who is forever praised" (vv. 24–25). The result of their idol worship was to fall into the pursuit of pleasure without a framework of relationship and redemption. The result of such a move was further degradation of their bodies and their humanity.

How often have we seen this in hyperreal culture—a relentless pursuit of pleasure as an end in itself? We know all too well the collapse into the desire for instant gratification without thought of consequence and the destruction it can bring. We see this destruction and degradation everywhere, be it the incredible rise of Internet pornography, the sheer volume of legal and illegal drug abuse in our culture, the personal debt crisis that is fueled by easy credit, the profligate spending of the hyperconsumer culture, and the obscene level of obesity in the West while so many starve in rest of the world. Thus, as Paul wrote, we exchange what God has given us, we throw away his truth for the lie; we bow down to the mirage of hyperreality.

This is something like the faith that many of us live today. On the surface we claim adherence to Christ. We may worship in church on Sunday, but deep down we know our allegiance and hope lie elsewhere.

NINE

Hyperreal Christianity

THE POST-CHRISTIAN TRINITY

Faith has been subverted and co-opted by the power of the hyperreal world. What we have now is a kind of hybrid faith that suits the goals of the hyperreal culture. I hope that through understanding this model you will begin the journey toward vital and life-changing faith. Let me explain through a diagram I call "The Post-Christian Trinity" (see p. 107). The model is in no way an attempt to explain the Christian idea of the Trinity; rather, it is an attempt to explain the way in which our spiritual beliefs interact with our hyperconsumer culture in a post-Christian world that no longer sees Christianity as a viable life choice.

THE DISTANT GOD

The diagram is a basic triangle. At the top of the triangle of the hyperreal framework of faith is the idea of the distant god. In our secular Western culture, many outside of faith still profess belief in a god. Often Christians hear this and are heartened, but what god are they speaking of? Something like Krishna?

Something like "the force" in Star Wars? People are not sure, as N.T. Wright explains: "The problem is that the word *god* or *God* simply does not mean the same to all people who use it: and, what is more, most people in Western culture today, when they use the word, do not have in mind what mainstream, well-thought-out Christianity has meant by it."[1] The main image of *god* that many people hold to is a distant god who is removed from the world, a sort of god whom people feel may exist, even though they have little or no idea of what he/she/it is like. Wright describes this view of god as a belief in a "far-off, detached being . . . remote, inaccessible and certainly not involved with the day-to-day life."[2]

The problem is that such a god can offer us no ethic of how to live. This is in deep contrast to Yahweh, the God of the Bible, about whom we can read. We can learn of his actions and attitudes throughout the history of Israel; and through the incarnation, we can see what kind of being God is. We can see that he is the God who wept over the lost of Jerusalem and who offered living water to a Samaritan woman. We can see that he is a God who loves humanity so much that he died on a cross, offering himself for the sins of humankind. But what sort of god is the distant god? What does such a god think of the suffering in the world? What does such a god think of sexual immorality, taxation, and fine art? We have no idea, and therefore such a god offers us no ethic, no way of living, no concept of right or wrong. With such a god we no longer even attempt to be good people; we simply aim to have a good time.

The Post-Christian Trinity

ME AS GOD

In the post-Christian trinity, authority does not rest with the distant god at the top of the triangle; rather, it rests with the individual. In our hyperreal culture, it is the individual who is the primary concern in all matters of life. The individual decides who he will relate to, how he will behave, and what he will believe. Demographer Bernard Salt, after studying in depth the way individuals see themselves today, described the new young adult culture as "the super-me generation: all that matters is me and my friends. 'I am at the centre of the universe and the world, and all its players revolve around me.'"[3]

With the distant god providing no direction or moral compass, the *super-me* individual must have an agenda for living. And with no voice from outside of the hyperreal culture offering advice, the only voice the individual hears is the constant mes-sages of hyperconsumerism—messages tailor-made to speak to the desires, wants, and needs of the individual and his personal life-project, messages that only further strengthen the belief that the individual is at the center of the universe.

CONSUMERISM AS FOLK RELIGION

The bottom right-hand corner of the post-Christian trinity tri-angle is the concept of consumerism as folk religion. We have already "outed" hyperconsumerism as an implicit or unspoken religion in our midst. Understanding the idea of folk religion will help us develop a deeper appreciation of the role con-sumerism plays in our spiritual lives. If you were to travel to a village in rural Indonesia and walk up to a farmer and ask him what his religion was, without a shadow of doubt, he would tell you that he is Muslim. However, if you were to stick around for a while and see the farmer's family in various life situations, such as his children taking exams, a relative falling ill, or his crops being destroyed by drought, that overtly Muslim farmer would not go to the mosque to pray, but instead he would engage in thoroughly pagan practices, such as the use of charms, astrology, and offerings to the gods that his ancestors worshiped before the Muslim missionaries arrived in his country. You would see the same in South and Central America, where Catholics will still hedge their bets, faithfully attending Mass but also praying to the old gods that predate Christianity's arrival in the Americas.

The reason people can live with two very different religions can be explained by the concept of two types of religion—high religion and folk religion. Anthropologist and missionary Paul Hiebert reflects on his experiences of relating to non-Western cultures:

> As missionaries we prepare to witness to people who are tied to Buddhism, Hinduism, Islam and other high religions which deal with questions of ultimate truth and meaning. We are surprised, therefore, when we find that most of the common folk do not know much about their own high religions, and that they are often more deeply involved in such folk-religious practices as magic, astrology, witchcraft, and spirit worship. We find that we are not prepared to deal with such practices.[4]

Therefore, despite the fact that many in the West may adhere to one of the major world religions, they probably know very little of the faith they claim adherence to and actually may be more involved with the folk religion of hyper-consumerism. This can be true even of those in the West who claim not to be religious, for high religion is ultimately about the big questions of life, such as: Where did we come from? How was the world created? What is the meaning of life? Scientific atheism has answers to all of these questions and therefore operates as a high religion. Folk religion does not concern itself with these big questions but instead focuses on the "everyday," as Hiebert makes clear: "Folk religions deal with the problem of everyday life, not with ultimate realities. Through omens, oracles, shamans, and prophets, they proved guidance to people facing uncertain futures. Through rituals and medicines, they counter such crises as droughts, earthquakes, floods, and plagues, as well as help bring success in marriage, in producing children, in business, and the like."[5]

With high religion's detachment from everyday life, it is then consumerism that speaks into the "everyday," offering us solutions, distractions, and hope that speaks into our pragmatic needs. But with these three elements in place of a distant god, the individual as god, and consumerism as folk religion, a vicious circle is created. With the distant god providing no ethic of living, with the individual ultimately serving self, and with consumerism both reinforcing this message and encouraging the individual to pursue materialism and hedonism without restraint, the individual then falls into a directionless downward spiral or addiction. Where does this downward spiral leave us?

All over the developed world, the reality TV program *Big Brother* has been a hit. Millions have watched a bunch of self-obsessed hedonists sit around discussing their sex lives and drug use. This is now entertainment. Ironically, what nobody notices is that although the show seems edgy, the contestants are actually imprisoned. They are captives in their prison of supposed pleasure. This is a powerful metaphor of life today; the lure of so-called freedom and pleasure hides the fact that we have all become prisoners of the self-entrapping nature of the post-Christian trinity.

THE HYPERREAL CHRISTIAN TRINITY

What does such a model of faith look like to those who claim allegiance to Jesus but live in the hyperreal culture? Sadly, it does not look much different. When I first began teaching about hyperreality, I found that I could not keep up with the demand. So many people wanted me to come and teach that I had to turn down most of the bookings. When I would teach at conferences, often my sessions would be overflowing. All this attention was not because I was some superteacher, but because I was talking about how faith dealt with their everyday lives. I would teach about how their faith interacted with the popular media in which they were immersed, how their cell phones changed their views of community and commitment, how their desires to travel were a form of self-serving pilgrimage.

People again and again would approach me after my talks and tell me that this was the first time they had heard teaching that was relevant to their real lives. Many preachers and churches would attempt to deal with everyday issues, but their efforts ended up looking like "Getting your finances in order God's way" or "How Jesus can help your marriage." This was simply not where young adults were at; these concepts were almost totally disconnected from their everyday lives. The concept of hyper-reality was their folk religion. It became clear to me why so many young adults were either leaving faith or finding their faith diminished: churches were making the same mistake that Western missionaries had made in their interactions with non-Western cultures' folk religions. Hiebert explains: "Given our

Western view of things, we do not take folk religions seriously. Consequently, we do not provide biblical answers to the everyday questions the people face. . . . It should not surprise us, therefore, that many young Christians continue to go to shamans and magicians to deal with such questions."[6]

The exact same thing is happening in the West, except young adults look to the shamans and magicians of the hyperreal culture—celebrities, rock stars, lifestyle magazines, supermodels, and advertisers. But what about Jesus? Don't Christians living in the hyperreal culture have Jesus to stop them from falling into this contemporary form of idolatry? Well, for Christians, the post-Christian trinity is exactly the same except that at the top of the triangle we replace the distant god with Jesus minus his authority over our lives. The reason Jesus has no authority is that we do not give it to him. In terms of authority we are just like the rest of culture: we still see authority lying with us. We still subconsciously look to consumerism as folk religion to deal with our everyday lives.

In a scene in Kevin Smith's irreverent religious satire *Dogma*, the Roman Catholic Church decides that the crucifix is an irrelevant symbol for today. They believe that the image of a half-naked man dying on a cross is not an appealing brand logo. Instead, they come up with what they call "Buddy Jesus." Buddy Jesus looks like a cross between a Sunday school picture book image of Jesus and an action hero. He is cartoonlike, winking and giving a thumbs-up sign. This is what Jesus without authority looks like in the hyperreal world. My friend Darryl Gardiner said this is Jesus as something like a "cool

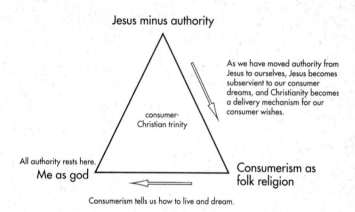

Jesus minus authority

As we have moved authority from Jesus to ourselves, Jesus becomes subservient to our consumer dreams, and Christianity becomes a delivery mechanism for our consumer wishes.

consumer-Christian trinity

All authority rests here.
Me as god

Consumerism as folk religion

Consumerism tells us how to live and dream.

waiter" in some hip café. He doesn't get too caught up in rules and simply wants you to have a good time. Research done in both the United States and Australia is backing up this view, revealing that young adults view God as something akin to a "cosmic butler"[7] to be called on in times of strife or need, but who then quietly exits so as not to cramp our style. Such a Jesus ultimately becomes subservient to us and our agenda. We rob him of his divinity, instead placing it upon ourselves. Jesus thus becomes the herald of lifestyle improvement; we follow him because he might be able to deliver us the consumer dream.

Such a Jesus is ultimately powerless to challenge the powers, principalities, and idols of our day. This is simply not a Jesus who can take us into a world beyond hyperreality. This is not a Jesus who can save us both in our lives now and after death. This is a Jesus who has nothing to say to the starving millions, to those trapped in prostitution, disease, and war. This is a Jesus with no plan for the world. This is a Jesus who has no good news. We need to rediscover Jesus. We need to discover the third reality—God's reality.

Part Three

God's Reality

TEN

Good-bye to the Plastic Jesus of Hyperreality

The starting point for understanding God's reality is Jesus. That's kind of obvious and cliché, you may think. But remember: if we just think of the Jesus that has been co-opted and made impotent by the hyperreal culture, we have the wrong savior. We need to reopen the Gospels and discover Jesus anew. For in Jesus we encounter God's plan to bring about his reality for the whole world. This encounter is essential if we are to understand the radical plan that God has for his world, a plan that will "save" the world.

For some of us, thinking about Jesus in a new light might be difficult if the Jesus we are used to has not delivered the kind of life we envisioned for ourselves. The problem is that many of us, without realizing it, have been carrying around in our heads a sort of "reduced" Jesus. This kind of Jesus might be good to call on occasionally when we have problems; he might be great for access on Sundays. But ultimately this "reduced" messiah has no chance of changing our lives, let alone the whole world. Maybe we did believe that Jesus wanted to make us a "success," but the more we have read of hyperreality, the more we have realized that what we thought was God's plan for our lives actually is the plan hyperreality has told us we must follow to be happy. Some of us may look back at the wonderful early days of our relationship with Jesus, wonder what happened, and ask, "Why has something that started so well just petered out?"

John the Baptist felt something like you may at this point. When he first met Jesus, he was full of excitement. He told everyone about the impact Jesus would have. He baptized the one he saw as the Messiah—the one Israel had been wishing for, praying for, groaning for. The one who would come to remove the oppressive Romans from their land. The one who would establish the nation of Israel at the center of world affairs, who would reestablish true worship at the temple, and who would usher in world peace. To John, the baptism of Jesus seemed like the happiest day of his life. God was finally intervening in the world, and things were going to change. You can hear the excitement and relief in John's voice as he said, "After me will come one who is more powerful than I, whose sandals I am not fit to carry. He will baptize you with the Holy Spirit and with fire" (Matt. 3:11).

But fast-forward and we encounter John again. This time, however, he seems like a different man. Unsure of what Jesus is up to, he sends his disciples to ask if he is the one Israel has been waiting for. "When John heard in prison what Christ was doing, he sent his disciples to ask him, 'Are you the one who was to come, or should we expect someone else?'" (Matt. 11:2–3). He was imprisoned by Herod; his unwavering belief in Jesus as Messiah had been shaken. He seemed to be thinking, *If this man is the "sent one," why are the Romans still in charge? Why has a new period of peace not been established? Why am I in jail? Is this Jesus who I thought he was?* John begins to think that he has been wrong about Jesus. He was sure that he had it figured out, but Jesus had other plans. Brad Young commented, "Whatever hopes John had for Jesus at the waters of the Jordan where he baptized so many, his expectations concerning the coming one were not being fulfilled in the ministry of Jesus."[1]

Sure, John was partly right about Jesus: he was the sent one, the Messiah. But things were happening differently than John expected. Like the other Jews of his day, John was not expecting the Messiah to be God; that was simply beyond their expectation. They were expecting the Messiah to be a man sent by God who would establish a wonderful period in Israel's history. But God was about to do something that nobody could even dare to imagine—God was showing up.

Like John's, our perceptions of what God is doing in our world have been shaped by a "reduced" view of Jesus. God is up to more than we can imagine. Sadly, John could not in his lifetime see the amazing way in which God was intervening in world history, for his imprisonment ended with execution. Our imprisonment is hyperreality. Will our captivity to the dreams of our culture stop us from seeing what God is doing in our world? Will our reduced view of Jesus stop us from gazing at his brilliance? Are we willing to leave behind our plastic Jesus and to explore the real Jesus—the Jesus who shows us the way to another world beyond hyperreality and our reality?

THE REVOLUTION BEGINS WITH BREAD

Let's dip our toes into the sea that is God's reality by starting with a weird subject—bread. In John's gospel we find Jesus interacting with a crowd that has come to hear his teaching. He is going back and forth, asking questions and telling stories as only rabbis can. The crowd asks him what they must do to please God. Jesus tells them to believe in him, the one God has sent. The people, however, want a sign, to which Jesus responds, "I am the bread of life. He who comes to me will never go hungry, and he who believes in me will never be thirsty. But as I told you, you have seen me and still you do not believe" (John 6:35–36).

The "bread of life" sounds like one of those classic Christian clichés. You know—the sorts of things you hear that go into the part of your brain that files away and then deletes boring and meaningless religious language. But we need to hear Jesus' words again. For it is with something as simple as bread that we begin to pull down the walls of the hyperreal culture.

As a boy, I liked white bread. When I thought of bread, I envisioned a loaf of sliced white bread that could be found in racks at the back of the supermarket. So, when I heard these words of Jesus, instantly an image of a loaf of sliced white bread came into my head. Bread was not a metaphor that could change how I saw Jesus. But one day my view of Jesus as the Bread of Life changed dramatically with a meal.

My friend Marko is Arabic; his family is of Lebanese and Syrian descent. For some time Marko had been telling me that he would like to cook our church community a Middle Eastern feast. We finally decided to take him up on his offer and invited whoever wanted to come along to one of our community homes.

Often the classic church community meal is pizza, because it is easy to order, it is fast, and is delivered to your door. It requires little or no commitment from the eater apart from contributing a few dollars to the cost and can be devoured in minutes. Marko's feast was different. It was an act of love, as for days Marko and his wife, Anne, had been preparing food. Upon his arrival Marko started grabbing people to help in the kitchen. This was not fast food; teams worked on various dishes, and the preparations took more than an hour, but no one complained. In fact, people enjoyed their roles. The team effort brought everyone together. As we sat down to eat, we surveyed the glorious feast before us laid out on a long table. Marko even got his grandmother on speakerphone to say grace in Arabic. People ate and laughed, enjoying the fruits of their labor.

As I sat back and reveled in the tastes and smells, I saw in the middle of the table pita bread. People were ripping off chunks of bread and dipping them in the hummus and baba ganoosh, filling their bread with lamb and tabouleh, mopping up their yogurt and kibbeh. As I looked around, I realized people seemed to have a glint in their eyes—this was true celebration. Then all of a sudden, I got it. This was the context in which Jesus referred to himself as the Bread of Life. He was saying that if people want to understand him, his purpose, and his mission, he has to be at the center. The bread in the middle of our table was at the center of this wonderful expression of community, allowing us to soak up all of the tastes and textures of the food. The bread was at the center of the laughter and joy. Those hearing Jesus would have gotten his metaphor right away. As Ravi Zacharias wrote, "To the Middle Eastern mind-set, bread is not just a source of nourishment. It is the bearer of so much more. . . . It is the means of friendship, celebration, and pleasure."[2]

By using the metaphor of bread, Jesus was outlining to those who were listening that his plan for our lives was extensive. Jesus was clear about his task of defeating death, sin, and evil by dying on the cross. Yet Jesus was also speaking through his actions, his words, and his life of another reality. Through an incredibly mundane object such as bread, Jesus was offering us a peek through the keyhole into a whole different reality that we can barely begin to imagine. Jesus' imagery offers us a few clear principles by which we can begin to understand his plan.

LIFE VERSUS ZOMBIE LIFE

By calling himself the Bread of Life, Jesus was highlighting his importance to our everyday lives. Many of us have given up on the concept of Jesus ever making a difference in our daily lives. He is a great form of cosmic fire insurance, but life is about getting on with it and making things happen ourselves. We might call on Jesus now and then when things go bad or when we want him to help us get something. Sure he was a great man and God and all that, but he did live two thousand years ago in another place that is a million miles away from our world of cell phones, Internet gambling, and lip gloss. Sure he said some nice things and some really wise things, but his parables and stories offer little or no direction in our twenty-first-century hyperreal culture. This view is typical of many Christians today, as Dallas Willard noted: "The most telling thing about the contemporary Christian is that he or she has no compelling sense that understanding of and conformity with the clear teachings of Christ is of any vital importance to his or her life, and certainly not that it is in any way essential."[3]

We do take clues from Christianity, but we tend to compile a list of the "nos" of faith. We construct a gospel of what we don't do. When I ask groups of Christian young adults what is different about the Christian lifestyle, the answers are always the same: "Christians don't have sex with the postman because they feel like it; they don't cheat on their taxes or do cocaine; they don't assault strangers with baseball bats . . ." What they are communicating is essentially a gospel that tells us how not to live rather than how to live. Therefore, we simply take our clues on how to live from the culture around us. As good disciples, we listen to our culture telling us what dreams we should have for our lives and then bring them to Jesus so as to "make them happen." Allen Wakabayashi explains:

The individualism of our culture has convinced many followers of Jesus that he will help us through every struggle and provide for our every need as we pursue our dreams. It's as if Jesus came to serve our needs; in reality, *we* are to serve *him*. Students often come to college all set with a vision for their lives—they imagine lucrative careers and upper-middle-class lifestyles. They've decided before their first year that they are going to be doctors or lawyers or whatever. So when they relate to Jesus, rather than coming with empty hands for him to fill with his dreams for them, they come with their hands full of their own dreams and say, "Jesus, please bless me as I go after my dreams."[4]

Then we find ourselves entrapped by the hyperreal dream. We become passive consumers, being entertained, following the well-worn paths of the hyperreal world. We slowly become less and less alive, moving toward a zombielike existence in which we must be shocked to be stimulated. Through Jesus' metaphor of himself as the Bread of Life, he speaks of a gospel in which he comes not to reduce life but to radically transform our real-time lives. This life transformation is not like the *lifestyle* enhancement offered to us by the hyperconsumer culture. Rather, Jesus makes the point that it is through connection to him and his *way of living* that we become truly alive. Jesus offers us a truly life-changing gift.

RECEIVING LIFE VERSUS CONSUMING IN ORDER TO FIND LIFE

Both in Jesus' time and today, bread represents a gift in Middle Eastern culture.[5] Today we speak of breaking bread together. Just as in our culture today coffee represents social connection, bread in Jesus' world and in the rich imagery of the Bible was a representation of hospitality. Enemies would mend their differences by eating together. When Jesus sent out his disciples to share his message, he told them to take no bread, as those who would accept his disciples would accept them with bread, a gift of peace and friendship.

Thus Jesus' offer of life comes to us as a free gift. This is truly radical concept in our hyperconsumer world. Jesus' offer is not something we must work in order to save up for; we do not have to buy it on credit only to have to pay later. Jesus' offer is free and available to anyone who begins to put his or her trust in his *way of living*. It is not exclusively available to a predetermined set of A-listers; there is no security at the door to keep out those who are not shiny, rich, and beautiful. Jesus' radical way is open to *anyone*—the broken, the depressed, the unimportant, the disabled, the forgotten, and the addicted. This is a message at total odds with the hyperreal culture. Slowly, piece by piece, we are seeing how Jesus' revolution of bread is beginning to uproot the myths of our day. For the *way of life* Jesus offers leads to satisfaction, not just more wanting.

SATISFACTION VERSUS WANTING

As we established earlier, our hyperconsumer culture is fueled by our dissatisfaction. We are trapped in an addictive cycle in which we must keep consuming and experiencing to be happy. Again, Jesus' message is drastically different from what we are told by our culture. When Jesus tells his disciples that he is the Bread of Life, he also tells them that whoever comes to him will never be hungry and those who believe in him will never be thirsty. Often we read this with our cultural lenses. We think of those around us who do not believe that Jesus ever really existed or suspect that claims about his life have been falsified. We also think of friends or family members who do not believe in a God or anything else beyond our physical world. Therefore, when we hear Jesus asking his listeners to believe in him, we imagine that he is asking them to believe in him as a concept, to accept the fact that he lived. On one hand, Jesus is asking those who are listening to believe that he is the Messiah and is sent by God. But there is more. Jesus is asking them to believe in his way of living, of acting; he is asking them to trust him and get on board with his way of doing things. He is asking the crowd if they trust him enough to model their lives after his.

Accepting Jesus as the Bread of Life would have been a lot easier in a sense if he were just asking his listeners to believe in him as a concept; they could accept that he was the Messiah sent by God. They could tuck away that abstract concept in their brains and then simply get on with their everyday lives. But Jesus was asking them to do something more—*to actually follow him.* By following he did not mean attending church, staying away from sin, and visiting the Christian bookstore occasionally. No, Jesus was telling them that if they really believed in him, they would do what he did; and by doing this they would find life both now and in eternity. The kind of life he was offering would actually lead to satisfaction. They would still have tough times and have to make sacrifices, but his way of life would lead to levels of pleasure and enjoyment they could never imagine.

REDEEMED PLEASURE VERSUS
DESTRUCTIVE ADDICTIONS

In Middle Eastern cuisine, bread is something that adds to and improves the quality of eating. Bread is used as a mopping-up tool, something that aids eaters in getting the most out of the taste of their food. Jesus, as the Bread of Life, aids us in getting the most out of life. He does not remove us from the ordinariness of existence; rather, he transforms our everyday life. We expect Jesus to arrive in our lives with bells and whistles; we expect our lives to be filled with earth-shattering experiences, with a sort of spiritual glamour. I have met people who have experienced supernatural encounters with God that have transformed their lives, but even those who experience such out-of-this world encounters must return to the mundane. But it is in the mundane that Jesus begins his program of subverting how we view life. We don't like this, for the hyperreal world tells us that things that are important are glitzy, loud, and astonishing. We want a God who flies around on magic carpets, shooting out lightning bolts and making mountains disappear and then reappear. We want a savior who acts like the hero of a fantasy or science-fiction novel. But that is the problem: fantasy is fantasy, and science fiction is fiction. Jesus begins where we live—in the ordinary. This is the revolutionary thing about Jesus: he gives us a key to unlock all that is good and pleasurable in this world; and unlike the hyperreal world, which tells us we must escape the ordinary to find pleasure, Jesus shows us how to find pleasure in the midst of real life.

By naming himself the Bread of Life, Jesus is placing himself in the middle of the feast. He is claiming that he is the glue that holds together all that is good and pleasurable. He is reminding us that all that is good flows from him, that this world was not just created as a holding place until we die but was created "good" and is filled with pleasure for us to enjoy. This is a difficult proposition for many of us to understand, especially those of us who are used to the "gospel of no" as our primary operating system or who have pictured Jesus as some sort of heavenly killjoy. To have such a view is to see the world through something other than the biblical worldview. The Jewish collection of rabbinical reflections on Scripture known as the Talmud says, "In the world to come, each of us will be called to account for all the good things God put on earth which we refused to enjoy."[6] We are called to communicate to others the goodness of God by enjoying that which is good.

John Piper has for many years written to convince Christians that their God-given role is to enjoy pleasure. Piper calls himself a "Christian hedonist" and has formulated a framework of Christian hedonism that is based around the following five tenets:

1. The longing to be happy is a universal human experience, and is good, not sinful.

2. We should never try to deny or resist our longing to be happy, as though it were a bad impulse. Instead we should seek to intensify this longing and nourish it with whatever will provide the deepest and most enduring satisfaction.

3. The deepest and most enduring happiness is found only in God.

4. The happiness we find in God reaches its consummation when it is shared with others in the manifold ways of love.

5. To the extent we try to abandon the pursuit of our own pleasure, we fail to honor God and love people. Or, to put it positively: the pursuit of pleasure is a necessary part of all worship and virtue. That is, *The chief end of man is to glorify God by enjoying him forever.*[7]

The biblical view of pleasure as echoed by Piper is in stark contrast to how the hyperreal culture views pleasure. Pleasure is seen in the hyperreal culture in one of three ways.

1. Pleasure is something that can help us escape the mundane nature of our lives.

2. Pleasure is to be pursued as an end in and of itself. Nothing else in life is worthwhile.

3. Pleasure is a masking agent that distracts us from the pain of life and the thought of our eventual deaths.

The hyperreal culture ends up turning something good into something that is ultimately destructive. When pleasure becomes an end in itself, disconnected from God, it turns into a destructive force in our lives. When we view pleasure as an escape from our lives, we need to live more and more outside

of our lives, an impossible task that leaves us socially disconnected and torn. This is how pleasure turns into addiction: the
quest for pleasure loses its sense of balance. For the addict there
can be no lows or plateaus; there can only be highs. But when
every moment is a high, the highs become the plateau; therefore new, more extreme highs must be found. The vicious
circle is complete. The gambling addict spends hours at the
fantasy world of the casino, the porn addict spends hours
online in a false world of unreal photoshopped sex, the drug
addict enters the chemical fantasy world of artificial highs.
When we view pleasure as all there is to life, not recognizing
the source of all pleasure as God, we become distanced from
God, cutting ourselves off from the main supply. When we use
pleasure to mask our pain, we only increase our pain, thus
needing bigger and bigger hits of pleasure to hide our pain. The
gift of pleasure that God has given us then turns into a negative force in our lives, as Harold Kushner explains:

> We have all seen people throw themselves into eating or
> drinking or sex or spending money, to such a degree that
> they no longer enjoy these things. The compulsive drinker,
> the compulsive philander soon gets to the point where he
> can't even enjoy his whiskey or sexual affairs. He keeps
> reaching for them only to still the pain, to make the need go
> away. But used properly, all of these appetites come to be
> seen as God's gifts to us, to add pleasure to our lives.[8]

Jesus thus offers us amazing freedom. By centering himself
as the giver of freedom, he reconnects us to the goodness of his

creation. He shows us a way that we can enjoy pleasure in our actual lives, and he links us to a way of enjoying redeeming pleasure and the pursuit of happiness. Pleasure then becomes a foretaste of God's reality. The more we place our dependence in God, the more we begin to experience his awesome plan for the world.

DEPENDENCE VERSUS CONTROL

The hyperreal world is all about trying to gain control over your life by making the right consumer choices. Jesus, however, asks us to take another way—the way of dependence. When Jesus used the metaphor of himself as the Bread of Life, he was making an allusion that every Jewish listener would have detected. He was comparing himself to manna, the bread God miraculously used to feed his people as they walked through the desert after escaping the slavery of Egypt. The Israelites found themselves forced to depend totally on God to provide for their every need.

Jesus was telling his listeners that he was like the bread that God had provided from heaven, and they were to leave behind their attempts to control their lives. His way would be the manna for their journey away from the slavery of self. All they needed in life was to connect themselves to him, and life would flow out of him. By putting their trust in other things, in themselves and their own efforts or in the idols of their day, they were choosing to cut themselves off from the giver of life. By putting all of their trust in *him,* they would be choosing to model themselves after the source of life—a source of life that was not just going to transform them as individuals but was going to transform their whole world.

FUTURE HOPE VERSUS MIRAGES OF THE FUTURE

The hyperreal world controls our actions and hopes by controlling our futures. We behave and put up with substandard lives because we are waiting for the *payoff*, that day when the hyperreal world rewards us with the perfect lifestyle. But this future is a pipe dream, a cruel mirage that means no matter how much we get or experience, we will always be driven to want more. Thus we become imprisoned by a future that will never turn up. By labeling himself the Bread of Life, Jesus shows us a radical view of the future, one that undermines the hyperreal world's grip on our imaginations. Bread pointed the Jewish mind first to the past but then to the future.

Jesus' Jewish listeners also would have picked up a nuance regarding bread that we could easily miss. Jesus' use of the metaphor of bread was a key to understanding his mission in the world. His Jewish peers would think of the matzo (unleavened) bread eaten each year at the Passover festival. The Passover festival was and still is celebrated annually to commemorate the deliverance of the Jews from their slavery in Egypt. The night before their deliverance, God told his people to prepare matzo bread. The bread was easily made and was light and long-lasting for traveling. By linking himself to this use of bread, Jesus was telling his audience that God was going to act in history again in the way he had in Egypt.

But there was another meaning: Jesus calling himself the Bread of Life also pointed to his mission—bringing about God's dream for the world, to have the whole world enveloped in God's reality. By using bread, Jesus reminds his listeners that God's reality will be ushered into the world via a feast. This magnificent arrival, this flowing of God's reality into our world would be ushered in by a feast! Those listening to Jesus describe himself as the Bread of Life would have grown up hearing the book of Isaiah read to them. The book describes the feast that ushers in the Day of the Lord, the coming of God's reality.

> On this mountain the LORD Almighty will prepare
>> a feast of rich food for all peoples,
>> a banquet of aged wine—
>> the best of meats and the finest of wines.
> On this mountain he will destroy
>> the shroud that enfolds all peoples,
>> the sheet that covers all nations;
>> he will swallow up death forever.
> The Sovereign LORD will wipe away the tears
>> from all faces;
> he will remove the disgrace of his people
>> from all the earth.
>> The LORD has spoken.
> In that day they will say,

"Surely this is our God;
we trusted in him, and he saved us.
This is the LORD, we trusted in him;
let us rejoice and be glad in his salvation" (25:6–9).

What an amazing concept! God ushers in the redemption of the world through a feast. By calling himself the Bread of Life, Jesus points toward a future in which God will make the world anew. He is not talking about the self-serving visions of the future that we are given by the hyperreal culture—visions of travel, house renovations, makeovers, or instant celebrity. He is talking about a future beyond comprehension—a future where the good guys win, where all that is wrong and evil is expunged from the earth, where pain and suffering are removed, where pleasure and goodness flow.

How can shallow promises of hyperreality compete with God's coming reality? To understand what this future will be like, we must look to Jesus, for he is a living sign of how the world will be transformed. He is like an explorer from a future civilization coming back in time to tell us what the future will be like, for this is a future unlike any we can imagine. And it is to the future we must travel next in our exploration of God's reality.

ELEVEN

A Fight for the Future

JESUS: CLUES FROM A WORLD REBORN

Jesus' life on earth points us toward the future. His actions act as clues showing us how the story of creation will continue in the future. Jesus' healing of the disabled points toward a time when humans will be healed physically and mentally. Jesus' deliverance of those possessed by evil demons points to a future when evil will be expelled from our world. Jesus' feeding of those without food is a glimpse of a future world when there will be no hunger, poverty, or starvation. By turning over the tables of the merchants selling religious products in the temple, Jesus shows us that the future will be a time when our worship of God will not be compromised by corruption and greed. Jesus' honoring of women, Samaritans, and children speaks of a time when no humans will be marginalized. Above all, Jesus' resurrection speaks of a time when death and suffering will be defeated and the world will be resurrected. Sadly though, most Christians miss these allusions, living as we do under the shadow of the hyperreal world.

THE WEAK HEAVEN

The more I speak at different churches, Bible colleges, and young adult ministries, the more I realize just how our lack of knowledge of what God is going to do in the future is controlling the lives of Christian young adults. Because I am not a youth pastor, minister, or lecturer, they are fairly honest with me. So I ask them, "What is the first word that comes to your mind when I say heaven?" The word most people come up with is *boring*. No matter where I speak, no matter what background or denomination the group, *boring* comes up again and again. This deeply shocks me. I think back to the accounts of Christian martyrs throughout history and in many countries today who would undergo torture and then death, steeled by their belief in the splendor of heaven and the life to come. For the groups I talk to, compared to the promises of the hyperreal world, their understanding of the Christian heaven simply does not cut it. Intrigued and determined to understand how Christian young adults are viewing their eternal future, I have begun to ask for more definite descriptions of heaven. They describe the following three versions of heaven.

Eternal worship singing. In this version of heaven, the general consensus is that people will spend the rest of their lives singing worship songs to God. Obviously this comes from a loose interpretation of the Bible describing heaven as a place of worship. This view of eternal singing seems to frighten even the most ardent worshiper that the future God has for us will be quite a boring place.

Clouds and harps. In this view of heaven, which is more based on cartoons and Hollywood films than the Bible, believers are taken away to a spiritual realm comprised of clouds and winged angels playing harps. This view seems equally unpalatable as the worship singing view to people who live and breathe in the real earth world. It struggles to compete with the readily available delights promised to us by the hyperreal world. (I was amazed by how many Christian people shared with me that their reference point for heaven was an episode of *The Simpsons!*)

Heaven as a personal amusement park. In this view, people see heaven as a spiritual realm created by God for them to do whatever they have always wanted to do. Here they win their favorite sports event, live on tropical islands, and eat whatever they want without putting on weight. This understanding of heaven displaces God as king of heaven, instead making the individual the king of his or her own personal realm. This view has more in common with some Mormon or extreme Islamic views of paradise, where believers are given that which they were denied on earth as a reward for abstaining during their lives.

These weak and unbiblical views of heaven are no match for a hyperreal culture that promises us a sort of heaven-on-earth "lifestyle." I believe this is one of the key reasons young adults are leaving the church; it is also one of the key reasons we struggle to reach young adults outside the church. Therefore, it is absolutely imperative that we rediscover what the Bible says about the future God has in store for us and how we

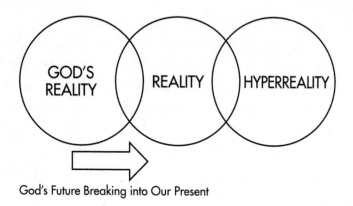

God's Future Breaking into Our Present

relate that truth to our everyday lives. For when we are talking about heaven, we are not talking about clouds and harps; we are talking about a future in which God's reality envelopes the world.

A NEW HEAVEN AND A NEW EARTH

One of the things that keeps our imaginations limited about heaven is that we simply cannot envision what it will be like; we are used to life as we know it on earth here and now. We struggle to put our hope in a world for which we have no reference point. How do we imagine life in a place we don't understand when we have never been there or met anyone who has? Randy Alcorn writes, "Everything pleasurable we know about life on Earth we have experienced through our senses. So, when Heaven is portrayed as beyond the reach of our senses, it doesn't invite us; instead, it alienates and even frightens us."[1]

Part of our difficulty comes from a misunderstanding of the biblical concept of heaven. I remember a few years ago while standing in a supermarket checkout lane, I noticed a copy of one of those crazy tabloid newspapers that feature all kinds of supposedly true stories. The headline of this edition was something like "Hubble Space Telescope Takes Picture of Heaven." The story claimed that NASA had taken a photograph of heaven. The obviously fake image featured what was a cloud city somewhere out beyond Pluto. As I laughed at the silliness of the story, I realized that this was how many understood heaven. By understanding our future home as a spiritual locale out there in space somewhere, we miss the finale to the whole story of the Bible.

Part of the reason we have seen heaven as a purely spiritual location can be found in the heresies that began to creep into the early church as converts from a Greek worldview brought nonbiblical influences into theology. The Greek worldview saw the physical world of matter and "things" as separate and inferior to the world of the "spiritual."[2] This created within Christian thought a distrust of matter and physicality. People looked at their bodies, creation, and the world as inferior at best and evil at worst. Therefore, believers influenced by this Greek worldview longed to escape this inferior and evil world of matter for the purely spiritual world of heaven. Such language is nowhere to be found in the Jewish worldview, which makes no distinction between the physical and the spiritual. In the Jewish worldview, the spiritual and the physical exist together; the world is not seen as inferior or evil, but as "very good" (Gen. 1:31). Therefore, the future the Bible promises believers is not about escaping the world of the physical; it is about the renewing of the earth as God intended it to be. It is not about leaving earth for heaven; it is about the reunification of heaven and earth.

WHAT IS HEAVEN THEN?

If our future is about the reunification of heaven and earth, what then is a biblical understanding of heaven? Theologian Millard Erickson writes, "Heaven is, first and foremost, the presence of God."[3] It is the place where God dwells and where his will is performed in fullness. We understand from the first verse of the Bible that heaven was created along with the earth at the beginning of creation. In the book of Genesis we read of God walking in his garden. This image points us back to a time when God moved freely in our world in communion with humans. Adam and Eve's choice to eat the fruit of the Tree of Knowledge of Good and Evil represents humans choosing to exercise our own will instead of living under God's will, choosing to reject God's reality and instead pursuing the construction of our own reality.

As heaven is God's reality—the place where his total goodness exists, humans' attempt to control our own wills—our lack of trust is shown for what it is: a rebellion against God's will. That excludes our entry into the heavenly dimension. Thus heaven, the place where God's will is done in full, exists alongside but separate from our reality. So, separate from God's reality, we face the consequences of pain, dislocation, loneliness, wrongdoing, suffering, and death. God, however, is not happy to sit by while the two realities remain separate. God is relational and desires to be reunited with us and with the rest of his creation.

As we read the historical events of the Bible, we see God again and again working to bring the two realities together. At various moments throughout the Bible, the space between the two realities becomes very thin. The Bible often illustrates this closeness with imagery of thunder, storms, fire, and lightning. We see this closeness as Moses encounters the burning bush; we see it on Mount Sinai as God gives the Torah to his people.

God chose the Israelites in order to form a holy nation from which his reality could pour forth. His desire was that they would become an advance guard of goodness and justice so as to prepare the world for the reconnection of the two realities. We see this closeness in the building of the temple, which was designed to be a sort of embassy for God's reality in our reality. God used prophets to act as ambassadors of his reality, reminding the people of the way things operate in his reality, telling the people that they must abandon the culture's evil, corruption, and injustice. But the people did not listen. So God broke into this reality in the form of Jesus. Through Jesus' death and resurrection, the major battle is won; the powers of this reality of death, evil, and suffering are defeated; and the final act of human history begins. It is in this final act that we live, awaiting history's ultimate finale, the return of Christ to this world to finally unite the two realities.

THE WORLD MADE NEW

So the radical future God has planned for us is not just about heaven; it is also about the renewing of the earth. The prophet Isaiah tells us of God's promise: "Behold, I will create new heavens and a new earth" (65:17). For many of us this is an expansion of the good news of Christianity. As Wayne Grudem notes, "Christians often talk about living with God 'in heaven' forever. This is not wrong, but in fact the biblical teaching is richer than that: It tells us that there will be a new heaven and a new earth—an entirely renewed creation—and we will live with God there."[4]

Our hope then is not that when we die we press the ejector seat button, expelling ourselves from this earth into a new "spiritual" realm. Rather, as believers, we have two pieces of good news: first, that when we die we will live with our loving God—Yahweh; and second, that we will live on a redeemed earth, as N. T. Wright makes clear:

> The Christian hope is not, then, despite popular impressions, that we will simply "go to heaven when we die." As far as it goes, that statement is all right; after death those who loved God will be with him, will be in his dimension. But the final Christian hope is that the two dimensions, heaven and earth, at present separated by a veil of invisibility caused by human rebellion, will be united together, so that there will be new heavens and a new earth.[5]

This integration of heaven and earth will see God descending to earth to dwell with humanity. The separation from God that humanity has felt will be rectified as God again walks among his people. We do not go to live with God; instead, God comes to live among us. The source of all goodness will be in our midst. The new earth will be not just our home but also the home of God. Randy Alcorn reflects on the imagery in the book of Revelation as the New Jerusalem comes down to earth from heaven: "Notice that the New Jerusalem, which was in Heaven, will come down out of Heaven from God. Where does it go? To the New Earth. From that time on, 'the dwelling of God' will be with redeemed mankind on Earth . . . Rather than our going up to live in God's home forever, God will come down to live in our home forever."[6]

To recap, we are talking about a vision of the future where God's reality floods into the earth, God comes to dwell on earth, and the world as we know it is reborn. But what does this look like? How are we to imagine our home reborn?

A WORLD REBORN

At a rational, intellectual level, we may struggle to imagine what our world would look like when flooded with God's reality. However, at an emotional subconscious heart level, we have an inkling. In his letter to Christians in Rome, Paul wrote, "For since the creation of the world God's invisible qualities—his eternal power and divine nature—have been clearly seen, being understood from what has been made, so that men are without excuse" (Rom. 1:20). Paul is affirming that in our human nature there is part of us that intuitively recognizes the work of God in our midst. This was made evident to me a few years ago when I was attending a conference in Capetown, South Africa.

Exhausted from the busy schedule and heady conversation of the gathering, I decided to take a short walk in a park not far from downtown. As I walked through this park, my head was down and my thoughts were full of the events of the conference. I looked up to see a springbok only a few feet in front of me. I had never seen such a creature outside of a nature documentary, and now here I was standing eye-to-eye with this magnificent animal. At such a moment, we realize that no words can capture what we are feeling. It is almost a physical sensation in our guts. Instinctively our jaws drop, and if we make any sound at all, it is a gasp. We have some words that we use to try to capture the essence of such a moment: *sublime, awesome, amazing.* But none of these words can adequately define what we experience.

We see this reaction in the way even the most cynical atheist will stand in awe while gazing across the Grand Canyon, or a group of teenagers brought up on a diet of computer games and television will stand in silence while watching a lightning storm. You may have had moments when you heard a piece of music that somehow managed to reach down into some deep, unknown part of your soul, leaving you speechless. Or on a rare occasion you may see someone so physically beautiful that you find your breath is taken away. Sometimes you will feel very small and insignificant as you look at millions of stars on view on a clear night.

A sense of awe can disarm and transform anyone. A few years ago I was visiting a prison for young offenders in northern California. I was with a ministry team that was going into the prison to spend some time with young gang members who had been convicted of gang-related offenses. Our team was made up of Franciscan monks and an ex-gang member who was now a social worker. I was the only non-Latino in the group, and as a six-foot-one Aussie with blondish-brown hair, I stuck out like a sore thumb. I jokingly asked one of the team members if I stood out and whether people would know I was an Aussie. He said to me laughingly, "Dude, you are going to stick out. . . . You don't look like an Aussie; you look like an undercover police officer!" *Great!* I thought as we entered the room in which we would hang out with the prisoners.

We entered the room first, and a few minutes later the inmates were led into the room. Instantly they noticed me. The ex-gang member and the monks seemed to have their respect, but for me they had only a barrage of sneers and looks that could kill. As the monks spoke to the group in Spanish, several scary-looking gang members kept their stares on me, flashing gang hand signs under the tables in my direction out of sight of their guards. I tried to ignore them. But everyone changed when the monk who was speaking said my name, along with the word *australiano*. The gang signs and sneers stopped, and the inmates transformed almost instantly from tough gangbangers back into the smiling teenage boys they were. Awe had taken over.

After the monk finished his talk, I was surrounded by the young men, who now wanted to shake my hand, ask me about kangaroos, and hear me say, "G'day." Most of the group had spent little time outside of their neighborhoods or prison. Many were illegal immigrants from Central America. They had never in their lives met someone from anywhere as exotic as Australia. Their sense of awe and wonder had been ignited, and just for a moment the eternal had entered the prison darkness.

As a culture, we have tried to downplay such feelings. The hyperreal culture tries to offer its own version of awe. Be it the not-to-be-missed TV event, the Hollywood blockbuster, or the once-in-a-lifetime concert experience, instead of awe we are simply given hype. For as Abraham Heschel wisely observed, "There is no answer in the world to man's amazement."[7] When we feel awe, we are reminded of the eternal destiny of our world. C. S. Lewis noted that humans pose feelings and desires that cannot be satisfied by this world or in this lifetime. For Lewis these longings were evidence of our being destined for another world.[8] Deep down we all have feelings to see a world devoid of evil and filled with beauty and unconditional love. Such feelings point to God's original intentions for our world. Novelist Chaim Potok is right to say, "Food, a melody, a sunset—all tell us of the presence of the sacred in the everyday world."[9] Such experiences become tastes of the world to come.

I once heard theologian Tom Wright give a lecture in

which he described the beauty we find in this world as some-thing like a beautiful bowl. We have the bowl, and we can recognize its exquisiteness, but we wait to see what the bowl will be filled with. This is like creation, a receptacle that waits to be filled with the glory of God's reality. This view of the future is one that we can at least begin to grasp. All we must do is imagine what our world would look like minus all of the negative effects of injustice, death, decay, wrongdoing, and pain. Alcorn's view is similar: "You don't need to look up at the clouds; you simply need to look around you and imag-ine what all this would be like without sin and death and suf-fering and corruption."[10]

Imagine for a moment God waving a giant magnet across the face of the earth. All that is wrong is drawn to the magnet and away from our earth. Pain, suffering, child abuse, death, disability, war, starvation, aging, anger, hatred, racism, vio-lence, loneliness, poverty, fear, insecurity, corruption, greed, and whatever else bad you can imagine is sucked away from our world out into space never to return. What an amazing place to live! Can you even begin to envision how wonderful it would be? The prophet Isaiah gives us a glimpse.

> "Behold, I will create
>> new heavens and a new earth.
> The former things will not be remembered,
>> nor will they come to mind.
> But be glad and rejoice forever
>> in what I will create,

for I will create Jerusalem to be a delight
    and its people a joy.
I will rejoice over Jerusalem
    and take delight in my people;
the sound of weeping and of crying
    will be heard in it no more.

"Never again will there be in it
    an infant who lives but a few days,
    or an old man who does not live out his years;
he who dies at a hundred
    will be thought a mere youth;
he who fails to reach a hundred
    will be considered accursed.
They will build houses and dwell in them;
    they will plant vineyards and eat their fruit.
No longer will they build houses and others live in
      them,
    or plant and others eat.
For as the days of a tree,
    so will be the days of my people;
my chosen ones will long enjoy
    the works of their hands.
They will not toil in vain
    or bear children doomed to misfortune;
for they will be a people blessed by the LORD,
    they and their descendants with them.

Before they call I will answer;
  while they are still speaking I will hear.
The wolf and the lamb will feed together,
  and the lion will eat straw like the ox,
but dust will be the serpent's food.
  They will neither harm nor destroy
on all my holy mountain,"
    says the LORD (65:17–25).

Now imagine God having removed all that is wrong from the earth. He again waves his hand across the earth, but this time he fills it with his glory. Think of everything good on earth being turned up, magnified, wonderfully exaggerated. Can we even dare to dream of such a future? Such a vision of God's reality coming across the world can only melt the plastic future of hyperreality.

A few hours before I wrote this passage, my pregnant wife called out to me across the house. She was lying on our bed, her face glowing. For the first time she had felt the movements of our unborn child. I placed my hand on her stomach and felt the faint flutter of my yet-to-be-born child. Palpably I felt that inexpressible sense of awe, a feeling that deeply connects me with the Creator. When we feel awe, sense beauty, thirst to make the world right, we are touching the fluttering movements of a world pregnant with God's reality.

WAITING FOR GOD'S REALITY

The problem with such feelings of awe, wonder, and amazement is that they pass. The concert lasts only for so long, the meal is finished, the sunset fades. The feelings of awe seem like cruel teasing, but such feelings are teasing only if they exist simply as brief moments of pleasure in a world going nowhere. These bittersweet feelings serve to remind us that we are in an "in-between" age. God has won his victory on the cross, and the world will be reborn; yet it is not fully reborn. Through my wife's belly I could feel the movement of my unborn child's legs, my wife could sense the baby's movement; and when we went to the doctor, we could see partial images on the ultrasound machine, yet we yearned to meet our child in fullness.

Even the seasons seem to remind us of this incompleteness. Spring comes after winter, and nature seems filled with potential; life bursts out everywhere. But then the cycle continues through summer and fall, and winter sets in again. The apostle Paul wrote that even creation and nature wait in this tension:

> The creation waits in eager expectation for the sons of God to be revealed. For the creation was subjected to frustration, not by its own choice, but by the will of the one who subjected it, in hope that the creation itself will be liberated from its bondage to decay and brought into the glorious freedom of the children of God.

We know that the whole creation has been groaning as in the pains of childbirth right up to the present time (Rom. 8:19–22).

The strange and wonderful thing is that this incompleteness allows us to put things in proper perspective. Understanding that the world is in the process of being reborn becomes a lens through which to view both hyperreality and day-to-day reality.

TWELVE

God's Reality Now

THE THIN CURTAIN BETWEEN HEAVEN AND EARTH

God's reality is not just a force that will invade our futures; what God is going to do in the future also reaches back into our reality today. Amazingly, Jesus' resurrection is beginning to break into our world now. To understand how God's reality relates to our lives today, we need to return to the Gospels.

At the beginning of Jesus' ministry, we find him attending synagogue. When the time came to read from Scripture, Jesus stood to read, strategically choosing the book of Isaiah. He could have chosen any of the many books of the Hebrew Scriptures to read that day, but he chose a volume filled with wonderful images of God's future healing of the world. From Isaiah's pages you can almost hear the groaning of God's people, desperate for God to invade the world with his reality. In Jesus' time, the words of the prophet Isaiah carried particular potency as the Jewish people looked for hope as they suffered under the brutal occupying force of the Roman Empire.

Of all of the people subjugated by the Romans, the Jews constantly caused their oppressors problems. Part of their resistance was due to the fact that the Jews held fervently to the idea of their one true God; they would not compromise their faith, unlike so many other cultures in the Roman world that were happy to mix and match their religions. The Jews also were buoyed by the belief that their God would come to their aid and rescue them as he had throughout history. Therefore the Romans had to put up with all kinds of opposition, ranging from political protests, to religious rebellions and movements, to full-scale military insurgency. So reading from a book that spoke of a day when Israel would be freed by God's reality breaking into history carried very obvious social and political overtones to those listening. Jesus read the following passage:

> The Spirit of the Sovereign LORD is on me,
> > because the LORD has anointed me
> > to preach good news to the poor.
> He has sent me to bind up the brokenhearted,
> > to proclaim freedom for the captives
> > and release from darkness for the prisoners,
> to proclaim the year of the LORD's favor (Isa. 61:1–2).

Luke told us that all eyes were transfixed as Jesus finished his reading and passed the scroll back to the attendant. Jesus then announced to the congregation, "Today this scripture is fulfilled in your hearing" (Luke 4:21). The crowd would have sat stunned at the implications of what Jesus was saying. By saying that the year of the Lord's favor was here, Jesus was proclaiming that not only was God now answering the prayers of generations and breaking into history to save his people, but he was actually doing this in their synagogue.

Still, the crowd's intrigue and shock would have been tempered with cynicism. How could the year of the Lord's favor be here when the Romans still patrolled the streets? How could God's reality be invading everyday life when Israel still sat in shame as a conquered land? Jesus' meaning probably evaded everyone listening that day, but Jesus was both fulfilling the prophecies about his coming and expanding the scope of God's redemption of the world.

The Jewish people were like believers today who ask, "How does the gospel affect my daily life?" They understand how the gospel is good news for what happens to them after they die, but they wonder how it affects their daily lives here and now. The Jews looked forward to God raising the dead to live with him forever, but they also were waiting for God's reality to invade their everyday lives in a powerful way. This is why the people listening to Jesus that day were so deeply impacted. Jesus was not only saying that God, through Jesus' life, was going to change the future; he was also declaring that the future was breaking into the present, and he, Jesus, was that breakthrough.

God's reality had not broken into the present in the complete fullness that it would in the future, but since Jesus' incarnation, it has been breaking out into our world. The problem today is that we do not have eyes to see it. We assess life with the wrong tools. We measure life, prosperity, satisfaction, and even the gospel with the tools of hyperreality rather than with

God's agenda. We need new ways of perceiving what God is doing in our world. We must understand how the curtain that separates heaven and earth is breaking down even in our day.

THE THIN SHEET SEPARATING EARTH AND HEAVEN

One easy way to understand how God's future is breaking into our reality is to imagine our world separated from heaven by a very thin sheet. As I have already mentioned, at times throughout the history of the Bible, such as at the liberation of the Israelites from Egypt, the delivery of the Torah on Mount Sinai, or Elijah's battle with the prophets of Baal, the curtain separating heaven and earth became almost translucent. Since Jesus' arrival in our world, however, that veil has become like a moth-eaten curtain, which, when held up to the light, allows tiny specks of light to break through. Sure, the curtain is still there, but the glory of heaven is beginning to shine through into our world.

Yes, darkness still covers the earth. In the last 150 years we have witnessed horror after horror, from world wars to genocide, disease, and starvation. Yet the holes in the curtain allow light to shine into our world. We often miss those points of light because they are off the radar of the hyperreal world. Such specks could be large-scale breakthroughs, such as the ending of apartheid in South Africa, or small-scale breakthroughs, such as a church cell group reaching out to welcome newly arrived refugees into their homes, or a truck driver deciding to follow Christ, or a wife forgiving her husband, or a group of

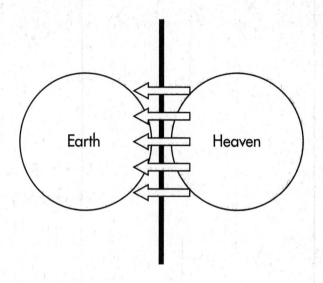

friends enjoying a great meal and realizing that all goodness flows from the Creator. Wherever we see justice, beauty, or goodness, there is a good chance the light is shining through from heaven.

During Jesus' time on earth, a sheet separating heaven and earth was imagery with which every Jew was familiar. Every child would have learned from his or her parents about the curtain in the temple, the holiest site in Judaism. This curtain (also known as the veil) separated the everyday parts of the temple from the ark of the covenant and the Holy of Holies. The Holy of Holies was the space in the temple in which God's glory (the *shekinah*) dwelled. Once a year, on the Day of Atonement (Yom Kippur), the high priest, having ritually purified himself, would go behind the curtain to make an offering for the sins of the people against each other and against God. In Matthew's gospel we read that at the moment Jesus died on the cross, the curtain in the temple tore from top to bottom. This ripping of the curtain that separated the Holy of Holies, God's dwelling place, from the everyday world, symbolizes the beginning of the tearing of the veil that separates heaven and earth. This act will reach its pinnacle at the return of Christ, when the veil is removed completely and God returns to earth to dwell, his will being done in fullness, in the reunification of heaven and earth. In the meantime, as we wait for the curtain to be removed, we can keep our eyes open for the places where the light is breaking through and the will of God is being done in fullness.

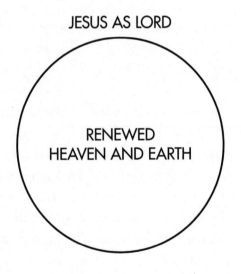

JESUS AS LORD

RENEWED
HEAVEN AND EARTH

HOLY VERSUS NOT HOLY

The idea of God breaking into our world in such a tangible way is revolutionary for many of us, especially for those brought up in a Christian culture that separates the world into the categories of holy and not holy. In this way of looking at the world, we can easily tell a "spiritual" activity from that which is "secular"—the world is divided neatly into two realms. Watching football would be secular; so would eating tacos with your best friend or starting a roofing company. Activities that would be "holy" or "spiritual" include going to a prayer meeting, practicing with the worship band for the Sunday service, or reading the Bible on the subway on the way to work.

This divide has become even stronger in the last few years with the growth of the Christian subculture. We have the secular punk band versus the Christian punk band (both sound almost the same, sans swearing), the secular gym versus the Christian gym, the rock festival versus the Christian rock festival, the theme park versus the Christian theme park, and so on.

As explained earlier, this way of looking at the world has little to do with a biblical worldview, but rather comes from the Greek worldview. That is why so often we miss what God is doing in the everyday world. We are used to God breaking into our world through an altar call at the end of a worship service, but we are not used to God breaking into our world through things in the everyday world. By labeling only certain activities spiritual, we have created a Christian ghetto, in which we restrict what God can do in our world, limiting our imaginations of how he can operate. We also then become blind to God's love letter to us—creation. I have often noted in my research with unchurched young adults how sometimes much more in tune they are with God's interaction through the world than Christians. We therefore need to recalibrate our vision; we need to become hunters of God's reality breaking into our world. But before we can truly appreciate what God is doing, we must understand how the pursuit of our own agenda and the pushing of our own will hamper our appreciation of what God is doing in our world.

GOD'S WILL AND HYPERREALITY

Surely, as God's reality flows into our world, no one would resist it. How could anyone be opposed to beauty, justice, and love? Regrettably, God's reality does find resistance; there are still areas that sit in darkness. Why is this so? The reason is that we still cling to our own agendas that run contrary to God's will for this world. The hyperreal world gains traction over our lives by encouraging us to extend our wills, by offering us the ability to control our world by gaining more money, buying the right products, and engaging in consumer experiences. As we have learned, such a worldview dehumanizes us; we become more self-focused, turning things, experiences, creation, and even others into products and commodities in order to serve our will.

The hyperreal culture celebrates the triumph of the will; we laud the individual who through sheer will can become a well-known success, and we reward such people with the title of "celebrities." Often, behind the scenes, the side effect of these people's rise to the top is a human trail of wreckage, of broken relationships, and manipulation. We see this phenomenon on the red carpet entrance of the Academy Awards ceremony each year. The actors walk down the carpet with small armies of personal assistants catering to their every whim. Media flocks to these stars, flattering them with praise to get them to stop and give short interviews. Star-struck celebrity chasers stand in the crowd, trying to get a glimpse of their idols (no pun intended), while a global audience of millions tunes in to watch the spectacle in an attempt to grab onto some vague notion of glitz and glamour. This is a world totally centered around the stars' will. Our culture worships such force of personal will. Go into any bookstore and you can buy biographies celebrating the way that stars have pushed their way over others to get to the top. And you can buy self-help books that will give you tips on how you can push your will in the same way. Just look at the way people operate in business, family, and politics. We are a culture that worships the individual exercising his or her will over others.

Unfortunately, our culture operates in direct contrast to the way God's reality operates. God is concerned with his will being done, and the exercising of his will comes through powerlessness. In Jesus' victory over death, hell, and the grave, the ultimate wielding of God's will comes through an act of self-sacrifice, of powerlessness. The Bible is the story of God wanting to extend his will to all creation, to make life on earth as it was meant to be. But God does not force his will upon us. His revolution occurs through the everyday and the ordinary; it begins not with the giant oak but with the tiny mustard seed. Therefore God's reality, the zone in which his will is done, invades our world not through violence but through love. Sure, it breaks through with power, but it is a power born of love and self-sacrifice. That is why God's reality is so often hard to see. We have grown up accustomed to looking through the lens of hyperreality; we expect amazing, shocking, and glamorous. So when God's reality breaks into our reality, we often miss it. And not only do we miss it, but we also resist it.

SURRENDERING OUR WILLS TO GOD'S FUTURE

One of the key challenges Jesus gave to his disciples was to give up their agendas, surrender their wills, and even put aside the wills of their families and loved ones. Jesus told his followers that to gain life they must give up their lives. For some of Jesus' followers, this became a literal commandment, by which they became martyrs for their commitment to Jesus. It is still a literal commandment for many followers who live in countries where believers are persecuted for their faith. For the rest of us, however, this giving up of our lives consists of surrendering our wills and laying them at Jesus' feet—along with our dreams, plans, and hopes. Such acts can frighten even the most passionate disciple, but really all we are doing is placing at Jesus' feet the hyperreal myth that we can "make it happen" ourselves. For

Jesus does not just ask us to give up our lives and surrender our wills. He tells us that by giving up our wills we will gain life.

This is where the journey out of hyperreality really begins. Giving up your life so that you may gain it runs contrary to almost every message about how to have a meaningful life we have received since the moment we were born. The hyperreal culture, so obsessed with making our lives a success, has missed the fact that the biblical imagination tells us not to chase happiness as an end in itself, but rather to follow God, to live according to his way. This is the road to happiness and meaning, as Rabbi Kushner explains:

> You don't become happy by pursuing happiness. You become happy by living a life that means something. The happiest people you know are probably not the richest or most famous, probably not the ones who work hardest at being happy by reading the articles and buying the books and latching on to the latest fads. I suspect that the happiest people you know are the ones who work at being kind, helpful, and reliable, and happiness sneaks into their lives while they are busy doing those things. You don't become happy by pursuing happiness. It is always a by-product, never a primary goal. Happiness is a butterfly—the more you chase it, the more it flies away from you and hides. But stop chasing it, put away your net and busy yourself with other, more productive things than the pursuit of personal happiness, and it will sneak up on you from behind and perch on your shoulder.[1]

So the incredible stress our culture places on pursing our own will and goals will not lead us to lives that deliver happiness. But the surrendering of our wills is not enough in itself to move us toward lives that are worth living. Jesus calls us not just to surrender our wills but to engage in a whole new way of living. This is the true essence of conversion, the giving up of our way of doing things and turning over control to the Creator of the universe. For this is where our concept of the future begins to break into our reality. We must let God's future set the agenda for our lives now. By recognizing that God is the Lord of our future, we give up the idea that we can "make" or "control" our future. By understanding that God's future is coming, we can only get alongside what he is doing, surrendering our wills at the feet of his future. The following examples show how what God is going to do in the future changes how we view the present.

A FUTURE OF JUSTICE

The Bible tells us that when God's reality breaks into our world, the earth will be filled with justice. Those who now go hungry will be fed; those who oppress the poor will be held accountable; those who are materially deprived will be blessed. If this is how the world will end up, we are compelled to act in the present. By getting alongside what God is doing now, we have a chance to partner with God as his reality breaks out into the world. We need to ensure that we are on God's side, for we have been largely shaped by the consumptive patterns of the hyperreal world. It is crucial that our way of living does not harm those who are on God's heart.

God's future is, as theologian Donald Kraybill called it, an upside-down kingdom. What Kraybill meant was that God's reality operates almost as a reverse image of this world. In God's reality those who are persecuted are blessed, those who are hungry now will be fed, and those who are oppressed will be held up. The upside-down kingdom applies to the rich as well as the poor. Those who are on the top of the pile in this world, those who have gained ascendancy while ignoring the poor, will find themselves at the bottom in God's coming reality. Therefore, if we call ourselves followers of Christ, we must follow his agenda, working alongside his plans. Working to alleviate material suffering and injustice in the world is an area in which God's reality palpably breaks into our world, and we must place ourselves at that cutting edge.

A FUTURE FREE OF SUPERFICIALITY

C. S. Lewis wrote *The Great Divorce* as an allegory of God's future. The protagonist in the book travels around the afterlife. In heaven he witnesses a procession that follows a beautiful woman. The narrator of the story seems to think that the woman is a well-known beauty, but in truth the woman is not known to many people on earth. She is just an ordinary woman by earthly standards, but her beauty and fame are not built upon earthly standards; instead, she is beautiful and honored because in God's future she is known by her character. During her mortal life on earth, she showed great kindness and godly love to all of those around her, even loving and taking in various stray animals. Her good works do not save her, but they do echo through eternity. On earth she is a nobody, but in heaven she is "one of the greats."[2]

Lewis uses the concept of the upside-down kingdom to reverse our obsession with superficiality. If the future is to be a time in which we will be known by our goodness and kindness, we must set about in the present to develop our character. The only life guides and teachers given to us by the hyperreal world are rock stars, supermodels, sports heroes, lifestyle gurus, and business tycoons; and all they can teach us is how to consume, how to chase after the material and the superficial. By imitating Christ and his way of life, however, we lose the addiction of superficiality and instead find depth, solidness of character, and peace of mind—all traits that will not only aid us in the world to come but that are invaluable in this world now.

A FUTURE BEYOND THE MATERIAL

As we have established, God's future is not about going to a "spiritual," disembodied ghost world. Yet how are we to account for the fact that Jesus sometimes seemed to speak against things of this world in favor of the eternal: "Do not store up for yourselves treasures on earth, where moth and rust destroy, and where thieves break in and steal. But store up for yourselves treasures in heaven, where moth and rust do not destroy, and where thieves do not break in and steal. For where your treasure is, there your heart will be also" (Matt. 6:19–21).

The Bible does speak positively of things that are material—wine, food, clothing, houses, and land are seen as blessings. But in God's reality these things are given their proper place in the order of creation. Actions, which have eternal value, are more important in God's future. This is what Jesus means by storing up treasures in heaven; actions and attitudes based in God's will for this world act as treasures both in this world and in the world to be remade. Attitudes and actions can bring either life or death. They therefore, in a sense, live on.

The fascinating thing is that this view espoused by Jesus over two thousand years ago is being rediscovered in our day by sociologists and psychologists in the field of happiness studies. Tim Kasser, who has extensively studied the way in which materialism makes people unhappy writes, "When people follow materialistic values and organize their lives around attaining wealth and possessions, they are essentially wasting their time as far as well-being is concerned. By concentrating on such a profitless style of life, they leave themselves little opportunity to pursue goals that could fulfill their needs and improve the quality of their lives."[3]

People who chase material goods find themselves less happy than those who pursue eternal and nonmaterial goals, such as relationships, altruism, spirituality, community building, and gratitude. Because God's future is coming, we must reconfigure our lives around goals that do not have material goods as the focus but instead reflect the eternal power and nature of God's reality. Doing so will not only move us alongside God's agenda for the world but will contribute to making us happier human beings. By following Jesus' example of living, we discover a tomorrow overflowing with peace.

A FUTURE OF PEACE

The Bible tells us that God's future will be a time of perfect peace. The Hebrew word used is *shalom*. In our culture we mainly use the term *peace* to describe a period without conflict or war. *Shalom*, however, means much more: it refers to a "rightness," "wholeness," or "completeness" in which all things are as they should be. It speaks of the perfect state of affairs as God desires them. It can also refer to "rightness" of relationship both in terms of humans' relationships with God and with each other. The idea of shalom also speaks of a time of fruitfulness and prosperity, in which people find themselves enjoying the benefits of creation. The book of Revelation describes God's people living in the New Jerusalem. The root of the word Jerusalem, *Salem*, is where we get the word *shalom*; thus we discover that those who follow God will find their home in God's perfect peace.

If this is the future that we are going to inhabit, how are we facilitating shalom in our lives today? If the future will be a time of perfect peace, how can we work toward building such a peace in our world today? What relationships do we need to restore to "rightness"? How can we work against conflict? How can we practice shalom toward our enemies? If God's reality is going to break into our future, it is essential that we wrestle with these issues, allowing shalom to break into our present and thus define our perception of reality.

By using the future as a lens to view reality, we begin to grasp what God is doing in our present. By focusing on the eternal realities of God's reality as it breaks into our everyday lives, we avoid falling into the trap of creating systems of control that run contrary to God's agenda. Once we lay down our wills before God, we must learn how to live within God's reality. We are all too familiar with how to live within hyperreality, but we need to learn how to live well within God's reality.

WISDOM, THE BRIDGE TO HAPPINESS

The concept of living well within God's reality in order to have a life of satisfaction and meaning was well known to Jesus and his Jewish peers. The Hebrew Scriptures (our Old Testament) contained a whole section of wisdom books, such as Proverbs, Job, and Ecclesiastes, that addressed how to live in the everyday world. These books gave guidance and instructions to readers to enable them to live lives filled with joy, happiness, fruitfulness, and meaning. The Jews called this bank of knowledge "wisdom." The Jews so valued this concept of wisdom that they spoke of it as almost an agent in the world, describing it as a holy woman moving among God's people. If we are to live a life of worth in the hyperreal world, if we are to be true to our calling as disciples, we must rediscover what it is to live with wisdom.

We have become estranged from the concept of wisdom. In fact, *wisdom* is possibly one of the most unappealing words in the hyperreal culture. People will spray themselves with fake tans, jog every morning, and diet for their summer bikini bodies, but nowhere in the hyperreal world will you find people with any real conviction seeking out wisdom.

We understand that older people may possess wisdom; but our culture marginalizes the elderly, not because we don't like them, but because we cannot imagine that people who have grown up without MP3 players and wireless Internet connections could tell us anything worthwhile about living in this world. But considering the evidence of what we have learned about the hyperreal world's inability to deliver us a life that is filled with true happiness, maybe the wisdom of past generations who have the ability of hindsight can lead us toward happiness in our own lives. Wisdom then becomes a beacon guiding us through the darkness of contemporary life. Wisdom becomes the guide for us, an alternate voice illuminating the way toward a life of meaning.

SIN AND WISDOM

Once we start talking about wisdom and right living, many of us start to feel a small pang of anxiety most likely caused by the way in which many of us have been taught about wrong behavior in the past. One of the reasons the word *sin* has gone out of vogue both inside and outside the church comes down to our understanding of how sin works. Many of us cannot help but think of God in the sky keeping a tab on our behavior the way a judge at a dog show does, looking out for the most minute indiscretions and unholy thought patterns in order to write them down in a giant book that will later be used against us. This may scare the living daylights out of us, resulting in a life wracked with fear and anxiety because we view God as a sort of schoolteacher tyrant.

Or as believers, we realize that we are going to get into heaven anyway and simply view sin as some sort of cosmic behavioral accounting that God does to amuse himself, which ultimately has no bearing on what we do in this life and will be wiped clean anyway. Therefore we sin away, only avoiding the really bad ones like murder, which could get us put away in jail. The result is that our lives behind closed doors look no different than the lives of those who do not follow Christ.

Ronald J. Sider's book, *The Scandal of the Evangelical Conscience*, confirms the sad way in which Christians' lives show very little transformation. Sider wrote, "Whether the issue is divorce, materialism, sexual promiscuity, racism, physical abuse in marriage, or neglect of a biblical worldview, the polling data point to widespread blatant disobedience of clear biblical moral demands on the part of people who allegedly are evangelical, born-again Christians."[4] This evidence proves that the wisdom books of the Bible are on the whole ignored. Christians in our culture don't see the Bible's instruction in behavior and living as having relevance. Both of these views of sin and Christian behavior therefore are miles from the reality of biblical Christianity.

God's reality is operating in our world. Since Christ's death on the cross, it has broken into our world. Therefore we must change our behavior to accommodate God's reality. God does not instruct us in how to behave because he is a cosmic killjoy determined to take the fun out of life. Rather, God labels some behavior as holy and other behavior as sin because of its effect on us and our ability to live within his reality and our everyday realities. The laws of God's reality are real; they are not simply abstract spiritual niceties.

E. Stanley Jones, a great twentieth-century statesman and missionary, noted that Jesus told his primary critics, the Pharisees, that the kingdom of God was within them. Jones said that Jesus was referring to the fact that the kingdom of God was a reality that operated in our world just as concretely as the reality of gravity. Jesus was telling the Pharisees that God's kingdom was inside them. Therefore, if they acted in sin, opposing the reality of God's rule in their lives, the consequences would be felt in this life, not just in eternity.

If we act in the ways of the kingdom, we will see benefits in our lives; but if we act against the kingdom, we will experience the fruit of that sin in ways that work against our happiness and well-being. Jones, writing in the 1940s, asked:

> Is the Kingdom of God then in us all, changed and un-changed? . . . The changed have related themselves to the laws of the Kingdom and to the God of the Kingdom, and therefore receive the resources of the Kingdom—the sum total of that Kingdom works with them and not against

them. Those who are unchanged find the Kingdom is within them, but they are at cross-purposes with it. In the changed person the Kingdom works as self-realization, and in the other as self-frustration. But in both it is there. The laws of our being are not other than the laws of God—they are the laws of God. These laws are not something imposed on the situation, but are written into the very structure of our being, into our tissues, our nerve cells, our bloodstream, into the total organization of our life. They are the way we are made to live . . . God has stamped within the structure of our being His Kingdom . . . If we live according to it, we live. If we don't, we don't.[5]

To sin, to choose to live in a way that runs contrary to God's reality, is to punish ourselves, to fight against the inherent laws of the universe as God has created them. Imagine trying to live against the laws of gravity. No one would dream of doing such a thing, for we know that to do so would mean at best a life of broken bones and bruises and at worst death of self and of others. So it is the same with the laws of God's reality. By following Jesus' example, we choose to bring God's reality into our everyday lives, filling our daily realities with "eternal" life. By choosing to live in a way that operates contrary to God's reality, we choose to bring the seeds of destruction, decay, and death into our everyday realities. The fruit of these choices may not be obvious to us because we live in the moment, viewing life through the lens of the hyperreal world. But if we look at our lives in their entirety, we can see the effect of these choices.

As I discover what scientists and psychologists are learning about what makes us happy, I have been amazed at the way in which the values and practices that make people happy fit like a glove with the concept of biblical wisdom. Sometimes when I speak to groups of Christian young adults about happiness, I put my Bible aside and say, "Let's forget Christianity for a moment and see what studies in happiness are telling us about how to be happy." I notice that people are intensely focused. They take out pens and start writing down what secular scientists are telling us about how to be happy. I then pick up my Bible and start reading from Matthew 5–7, where Jesus gives his Sermon on the Mount, his manifesto for living. I don't even have to spell it out; I can see the shock on their faces as they realize that Jesus is saying the same thing as the happiness experts. People start to realize that the gospel has more to say to us than how to get to heaven and how to avoid sin.

We therefore need to view God's instructions for life not as a guide to eternal scorekeeping, but rather as a guide to living well. The book of Proverbs uses the metaphor of an adulterous woman to describe the lure of choosing to live contrary to God's reality:

> It [wisdom] will save you also from the adulteress,
>> from the wayward wife with her seductive words,
> who has left the partner of her youth
>> and ignored the covenant she made before God.
> For her house leads down to death
>> and her paths to the spirits of the dead.

> None who go to her return
>> or attain the paths of life. (2:16–19)

Note that the passage makes clear that those who choose to ignore God's instruction and choose to be seduced by the temptations of living against God's law will not attain the paths of life. They will bring destruction upon themselves.

The medieval spiritual writer Teresa of Avila had a powerful metaphor to describe the effects of choosing sin over wisdom. She described the spiritual life as a journey toward a castle through a series of courtyards. The disciple would move through these courtyards until he reached the center of the castle, which represented perfection. Each courtyard was different and portrayed a different stage of spiritual growth. But for those who chose not even to begin the journey, life was lived outside the castle among the frogs and reptiles who lived in the darkness. Teresa wrote of those who stayed outside: "There are souls so infirm and so accustomed to busying themselves with outside affairs that nothing can be done for them, and it seems as though they are incapable of entering within themselves at all. So accustomed have they grown to living all the time with the reptiles and other creatures to be found in the outer court of the castle that they have almost become like them."[6]

Teresa was making a crucial point that is just as relevant to us today as when she wrote it in the sixteenth century. The effect of not living according to God's instruction and wisdom is to cut yourself off from the fount of all goodness; it is to remove yourself from the source of your humanity. Just like those "souls" who became like the reptiles in Teresa's allegory, if we put our hope and trust in hyperreality, we will become like hyperreality and bring its values down upon us. If we live only looking at the surface, we will lose our depth, becoming superficial. If we live by consuming products, we will become products ourselves. If we treat relationships as commodities, we will end up lonely.

By embracing hyperreality, we embrace the destruction it brings. Therefore, biblical warnings regarding sin and foolish living are warnings against life-destroying habits. The Bible is like an owner's manual of life; it tells us how to act, how to live lives that reflect God's reality in this life, which is the essence of wisdom. Those who wish to live lives of meaning, fruitfulness, and happiness are encouraged by the writer of the following proverb to follow the holy woman, who represents wisdom and right living, not the adulterous woman.

Blessed is the man who finds wisdom,
> the man who gains understanding,
for she is more profitable than silver
> and yields better returns than gold.
She is more precious than rubies;
> nothing you desire can compare with her.
Long life is in her right hand;
> in her left hand are riches and honor.
Her ways are pleasant ways,
> and all her paths are peace.

She is a tree of life to those who embrace her;
>   those who lay hold of her will be blessed (Prov. 3:13–18).

Those who choose to live according to God's reality, who pursue wisdom, find life. It is fascinating to observe verse 18, which says those who seek to live in a wise way hold on to the "tree of life." We find the Tree of Life in the center of the garden of Eden in the book of Genesis. It represents the eternal connecting point humanity had to God and his good creation. The tree also represents the fruitfulness that those who follow Christ and imitate his ways will find in their lives. And it is eerily reminiscent of the tree we find at the end of the Bible as well, radiating from the center of the New Jerusalem. The tree is our future, and it represents humanity's hope.

THIRTEEN

Six Keys to Living Well
Within God's Reality

1. EXAMINE YOUR LIFE WITH FEARLESS HONESTY

One of the first steps people who join Alcoholics Anonymous take is to make a fearless and searching moral inventory of their lives. They are asked to spend a significant amount of time looking back over their lives and examining the way in which they have lived and acted. They consider the resentments and hurts they have held and the way these hurts and dysfunctions have resulted in the harming of others.

To truly find our way out of hyperreality and into the freedom of God's reality, we need to take a similar fearless and searching inventory of how we have let hyperreality affect our lives, for change as Jesus taught us comes at a heart level. We need to examine our hearts, our deepest feelings and dysfunctions, those parts of ourselves that are preyed upon by the hyperreal culture. If we fail to deal with hyperreality at a heart level, all we have learned about hyperreality will simply be information to be ignored or forgotten.

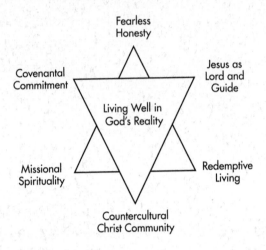

Over the last few years, I have spoken to hundreds of people about hyperreality, and many others have interacted with my teaching through listening to my talks on CD and through *The Trouble with Paris* DVD resource.[1] Many of these people contact me by e-mail or approach me in person to share with me how they are doing in their attempts to become free of the trap of the hyperreal world. I have noticed that it is those who really get their fingers into the painful parts of their lives, those who search out the dysfunctions and disappointments that give the hyperreal world a foothold in their lives, are the ones who are most able to find new life in their everyday lives by interacting with God's reality. Therefore, it is imperative that we spend time meditating honestly on the following questions.

These questions are not designed to make you feel bad or to feel any better or worse than others. Although I have spent the last four years speaking and teaching about the dangers of hyperreality, I find that it creeps into my life constantly. Often I am embarrassed at the way I have been sucker punched by the hyperreal world. So, in my life I have developed a process of constant self-examination:

- In what ways has my hope been dictated by the hyperreal world?

- How do I try to escape reality?

- In what ways have I been shaped by the hyperreal world? How has this shaping affected my behavior?

- How has the hyperreal culture affected my ability to commit?

- How has the hyperreal culture affected the way I enter into relationships?

- How has the hyperreal culture affected the way I engage with Christian community?

- How has the hyperreal culture affected my sexuality?

- How has the hyperreal culture affected my values?

- How has hyperconsumerism shaped my behavior?

- How has the hyperreal culture affected my discipleship?

- How do I attempt to control my life?

- How have I valued surface over depth?

✦ In what ways have I tried to pursue happiness through means that are outside of God's reality?

✦ What particular idols of the hyperreal culture do I worship in my life?

✦ What dysfunctions, disappointments, and hurts do I have in my life that allow the hyperreal culture to gain a foothold?

Spend time working through these questions with someone you trust. Without a relationship of accountability, it is almost impossible to escape the temptations of the hyperreal culture. For some people, issues raised particularly around pain, past hurts, and dysfunctions mean that you might need to invest in speaking with a licensed professional. Such a process as this can be very raw. After completing this process, many people find themselves lost, wounded, or out of control. But it is at this point that God can begin reconstructing us. For this is the beginning of the repentance that Jesus calls us to—a repentance that takes seriously the ways in which we have looked for control outside of God, a repentance rooted in fearless and searching self-honesty. Only after we have taken this inventory can we move on to living within God's reality.

2. BATHE IN THE SATISFACTION OF COVENANTAL RELATIONSHIPS

To find happiness, to find lives that run parallel to God's reality, we need to rediscover the joy that comes from covenantal relationships. Sadly, many of us have no idea what covenantal relationships look like. This is because the hyperreal culture has played down any positives that could come out of a committed relationship. The most common sex scene you see on TV or in the movies is an encounter between strangers. You know the one—two people who barely know each other are drawn to each other through pure animal magnetism. Glances are exchanged across the room, flirting signals intension, and the first chance these strangers get to be alone, they engage in wild cinematic sex. Our culture has eroticized the stranger. We don't just see this phenomenon on the screen; we see it in our own lives. We find ourselves lusting after or having crushes on people we barely know, whether it be the model in the makeup ad, someone at the bus stop, or the gardener. The stranger speaks to us of excitement, danger, passion, and wild sexual abandon.

Conversely, we view commitment and familiarity as uninspired, boring, and mundane. We almost believe that as soon as we are committed to something or someone, we take away the ability of that thing or person to excite us and draw us in. But when we look beyond the mythology of our culture and examine the actual hard evidence, we find that it is not the young, single people engaging in random sexual encounters who have the best sex lives. Those who have studied happiness tell us, "Married people . . . have better sex lives on average than single people—more of it more satisfying."[2] Why is this so? The research tells us that the best environment for satisfying sex lives is within a stable, committed marriage. Interestingly, we learn, "Though cohabitation is becoming much more common, it has not so far proved as stable a form of relationship as marriage."[3] This is because covenant is the habitat of the erotic; commitment is the environment in which pleasure can best be enjoyed.

God's original home for humanity was the garden of Eden, which until the Fall was a place of commitment and covenant, in which God, humanity, and creation were in perfect relationship. If we look at the story of the Bible, we find the thread of covenant and commitment running through almost every book. Nowhere is this illustrated more vividly than in the book of Hosea. Hosea was God's man of his time. He was called to be a prophet and to speak God's agenda into the public sphere. We can speculate on what sort of wife such a public spiritual leader would need—dependable, loving, devoted, holy. Instead, God told Hosea to wed a prostitute. His choice was Gomer, who betrayed Hosea again and again. To the untrained eye this seems like a strange choice, but God used Hosea's life as a living metaphor of his relationship with the people of God. Hosea represented God, and Gomer represented God's people, who continuously betrayed him, giving in to temptation and breaking relationship. In a beautifully moving passage, speaking as a betrayed husband, God speaks of his desire to woo back his adulterous lover.

"Therefore I am now going to allure her;
    I will lead her into the desert
    and speak tenderly to her.
There I will give her back her vineyards,
    and will make the Valley of Achor a door of hope.

There she will sing as in the days of her youth,
>   as in the day she came up out of Egypt.
"In that day," declares the LORD,
>   "you will call me 'my husband';
>   you will no longer call me 'my master'" (Hos. 2:14–16).

In this passage we see the wonder of a covenantal relationship. Because of his wife's unfaithfulness, God could reject her. But instead, in the spirit of unconditional love, he chooses to win her back, not only alluring her, but restoring her, healing her, and making her whole. The Bible often refers to marriage as an example of God's covenantal love to his people. This covenant is different from the contractual way of life espoused by the hyperreal world, in which parties hold back on committing in order to get the "most out of a deal." Covenant, rather is based on submission, unconditional love, sacrifice, and fidelity.

It is interesting that Christians will often pay strict adherence to fidelity when it comes to sexual ethics. Millions of dollars and countless man hours have been spent convincing Christian youth and young adults not to engage in sex before marriage. This is not a bad thing, because at the heart of Christian sexuality is covenant and fidelity. But often we forget any Christian ethic of fidelity and covenant when it comes to other kinds of relationships. We show little commitment to our neighborhoods and communities, our extended families, our churches, the poor, those outside of faith, and our enemies. Instead of being shaped by the biblical covenant, we are shaped by hyperconsumerism and radical individualism. We are called to be sexually faithful and committed, but we are also called to be just as committed and faithful in the whole gamut of human relationships.

One of the wonderful things about Jesus' life on earth is the way he was able to foster positive and life-affirming relationships with just about anyone he met. The tax collector, the Roman officer, the leper, and the prostitute found themselves, when in contact with Jesus, engaging in humanizing relationship. One of the first things Jesus did in his ministry was create a band of disciples. He assembled a disparate, ragtag group who, despite their obvious shortcomings, embodied covenantal commitment to one another.

God's reality is all about the restoration of relationships and the fostering of a new way of relating to one another. The time of the shalom of righteousness is upon us, and by moving alongside that, we find meaning. The good news is that the more we engage in covenantal relationships, the happier we will be. Social commentator Clive Hamilton wrote, "People who can name several intimate friends are healthier and happier than those who have few or no close friends." Psychologist Barry Schwartz's research points out that it is not just having close friends that makes us happier, but having a variety of relationships that contribute to our well-being:

What seems to be the most important factor in providing happiness is close social relations. People who are married, who have good friends, and who are close to their families are happier than those who are not. People who participate in religious communities are happier than those who do not.

Being connected to others seems to be much more important to subjective well-being than being rich.[4]

Therefore, people who invest time in building a variety of
relationships in all areas of life find themselves happier. Political
scientist Robert Putnam's book, *Bowling Alone*, charts the way
in which the diminishment of community relationships has led
to an overall drop in the quality of relationships.[5] Putnam notes
that even how much you commute and travel away from your
home has a direct effect on your ability to engage in and enjoy
community, which then limits your ability to be happy.
Modeling covenant in our relationships is vital for Christians,
for the hyperreal world tries to move us away from committed
connected relationships. It encourages singles to hold off for a
better deal, couples not to commit, and the married to leave
marriage if it does not serve their needs. It also encourages us
to compete with our neighbors, to pull back in fear from the
poor, and to hate our enemies.

I recently attended a conference for churches ministering
in urban areas. I heard a Salvation Army officer share that one
of the emerging ministries for her organization is to care for
single urban dwellers who die alone in their well-furnished,
gadget-rich, inner-city apartments; she said that it is normal for
these people to remain dead and unfound for weeks, as nobody
knows that they have passed away, so loose and liquid is their
web of uncommitted relationships.

The endgame of radical individualism is dying alone and
lonely. We must model an alternative. We are called to bring a

new vision of relationship into the world. Therefore, if you are to live well within God's reality, it is essential that you build positive, committed covenantal relationships in all spheres of life.

3. ENJOY A MISSION BIGGER THAN YOURSELF

People who are happy are people who are part of a struggle or mission that is bigger than themselves. Happiness studies show that people whose only life goal is personal material gain or personal achievement end up frustrated and unhappy. Thus the road to happiness is filled with involvement in activities that promote the greater good. People who participate in volunteerism, community building, and justice work do so because they are passionate about causes; they are motivated to help others. A wonderful by-product of such altruistic pursuits is the sense of significance, meaning, satisfaction, and happiness that accompanies living for a mission bigger than oneself. We do not engage in such pursuits simply to get happy, but there is also no point, in a hyperreal culture that encourages us to chase our own dreams, to hide the fact that by helping others we discover peace and meaning.

This dynamic also works out in terms of religion. Happiness studies tell us "that people who believe in God are happier."[6] But we also find that it is not just "having" religion that makes us happier. It is how we approach religion that determines how it will positively or negatively affect our lives. Some fascinating research into the links between happiness and religious belief have determined that some forms of religious belief can be harmful to one's levels of well-being and happiness.[7] The critical difference is how one approaches religion.

If you approach faith as a means to simply make your life better or to advance your personal agenda, you will find religion harmful to your personal happiness. But if you approach religion with a framework that is rooted in seeing faith as an all-encompassing way of life, something that you devote yourself to in a spirit of sacrifice and submission, you will find that religion has a profound effect on your happiness. This is a huge wake-up call to a contemporary Christian culture that has at best couched the gospel in a casing of self-improvement and at worst as a Christian version of the consumer lifestyle package.

Again we are brought back to God's reality working in our lives. God is not satisfied to remain static; he burns with passion to see the world made anew. When we join him in this quest, we find ourselves moving with God's reality; but when we pursue our own selfish hyperreal goals, we work against his purpose. The result is that goodness and fruitfulness flow into our lives. We must rediscover what it is to live lives of mission.

We are not used to enjoying the fruit that comes from engaging in mission. We are used to desiring the plastic trinkets of hyperreality. But when we engage in mission, unimaginable rivers of goodness can begin to flow into our lives. The problem, however, is that many of us have given up on communicating our faith in this world. Maybe we are stuck in the cycle of pagan envy, of not wanting to rob our friends of the promised pleasures of the hyperreal culture. Or it could be that we have become disillusioned by the models of mission we have seen, models that seem to push a belief system onto others who have no interest. We need to reconnect with a biblical understanding of mission in the light of God's reality breaking into the world.

When Jesus began his mission, he proclaimed the year of the Lord's favor. This was like announcing to a condemned prisoner moments before his execution that the governor had given him an unconditional pardon. This was what everyone in Israel wanted—God coming into the world to remake it, minus all the bad stuff. The repentance that Jesus called his followers to was more of a reorientation. Today when we hear the word *repentance*, we imagine altar calls or admissions of sexual sin. But Jesus was inviting his listeners to jump off the express train to destruction in the everyday and join his freedom train to a world reborn. Jesus did not hide the fact that such a total reorientation of life was going to be difficult, but he was just as adamant that by following him, people could access "eternal life" in the present. Therefore, when we talk about mission, we are inviting people to a present way of life into which God's reality is breaking out and a future in which the world will be remade in total perfection.

We can see now why in the Gospels when Matthew the tax collector decided to reorient his life around God's reality Jesus and his friends threw a party. Mission in the early church was not a solemn plan devised at some Jerusalem-based denominational headquarters. Rather, as early church expert Michael Green describes, "It was a spontaneous movement arising from Christian men who could not keep quiet about Jesus their

Lord."[8] The gospel poured from a handful of followers in Jerusalem out into the lives of millions in the Roman world through the transformative effect Jesus' way of living had upon lives. Missiologist Lesslie Newbigin described it as "a vast explosion of love, joy and hope realized in the world by the resurrection from the tomb of the crucified and rejected Jesus. The shock waves of that explosion spread within a few years to all quarters of the compass."[9]

Even in the face of torture and persecution, people could not hold inside what had happened to them. They had uncovered the myth of their day: the cult of Rome could not give them present and eternal salvation. Jesus—not Caesar—was Lord, and he had been resurrected from the dead. Moreover, that resurrection power was breaking out into their everyday lives. Thus it should be for us today. We are inviting people to a future in which the world is reborn, in which all of our deepest needs are answered. We are called to model to the world a way of life in which we exemplify a new way of living that is rooted in God's reality. We must be people who live the good news of the coming of God's reality into our world, not just people who talk about good news.

Mission also moves us toward getting alongside what God is doing among the poor, the broken, and the marginalized. My first ministry training was with the Salvation Army. I had grand dreams of being a pastor, but my mentor first put me to work serving lunch to the homeless and mentally ill. I was a teenager and devastated by the fact that instead of learning how to preach, I would be dealing with people of whom, quite frankly,

I was afraid. But through delivering soup and donated bread to people who struggled with schizophrenia, I learned vital lessons in living well within God's reality. I learned that the poor were not simply a demographic, but that these were people just like me, that they could be great fun, that they could be my friends. But most of all, I learned that many poor and marginalized people are incredibly close to God.

I cannot explain why theologically, but when I have ministered to the poor, I have sensed almost palpably God's Spirit in ways I never have in worship services and prayer meetings. Most of all, I am again and again shocked that when I am in relationship with the poor, I find myself being ministered to, encouraged by, shown hospitality to, and taught by people who the hyperreal world says have nothing to say, but who are the "stars" of God's reality. I don't want to romanticize ministry among the poor; I have been ignored, insulted, manipulated, and physically endangered. But God dwells in a special way among those who are on the margins of our hyperreal culture, those who are truly wise, because through their experience they can see the lies our culture tells.

Recently I had a time when I felt very far from God. During this wilderness I was invited to speak at a large church's youth service. The young people put on a cutting-edge, hip service. The kids moshed, jumped, and break-danced while a DJ mixed for the punked-up worship; and video and multimedia images were used to create just the right atmosphere. I got up to speak and did my usual "cool" preaching shtick, dropping references to TV, music, and popular culture. When it came to preaching up a storm for the kids, I thought I did pretty well. But the darkness that had been hanging over my life still hovered above me.

As I headed for my car, I was stopped by a man in an electric wheelchair. He wanted to talk to me, and although I just wanted to get home, I sat down to listen to him. In an accident in his youth, he had acquired a brain injury that had robbed him of the use of much of his body. Through his gray beard he spoke to me in stammered speech that was almost inaudible. For twenty minutes we sat there as he shared with me how he viewed his life as a miracle of God. He could have spent his entire life in a coma, but he felt that he had been saved by Jesus, and he was extremely thankful to have the life he had. As he spoke, I inexplicably felt my own darkness lift. I thanked him for ministering to me. As I got into my car, I watched him drive off slowly in his wheelchair down a deserted alley covered in trash and graffiti.

This man, according to the harsh and marginalizing standards of our hyperreal culture, was irrelevant. He was old, poor, and disabled, everything we deeply fear. Tears streamed down my face as I realized that I followed a magnificently surprising God, and that by becoming friends with Jesus' friends, my life is made immeasurably richer. The poor and marginalized can be wonderful guides and mentors who are able to lead us out of the traps of hyperreality.

4. FOLLOW JESUS AS LORD AND GUIDE

I mentioned earlier that Jesus' revolution begins with our hearts. Now, many of us would admit that Jesus has entered into our hearts. But often when we use this language, we are speaking of the way in which we keep our faith private inside of ourselves. The hyperreal culture is happy for people to be religious as long as they keep their beliefs private and out of the public sphere. By using the language of Jesus being in our hearts, we can fall into the trap of hiding away our faith.

In many ways, this situation is similar to the early Christian movement. The Roman culture was happy for people to believe anything they wanted to in the religious and cultural melting pot, as long as at the end of the day they bowed before the emperor, who was the symbol of the Roman system. They were told that behind closed doors, in temples and homes, they could worship in any way they wanted as long as they kept it out of the public sphere. For the many different religions of the Roman world, this was a good compromise. They could do what they wanted as long as they bowed before Caesar. But this is where the early Jesus movement proved to be different from the other religions. The Jesus followers refused to bow before Caesar and to keep their faith hidden away in the cupboard. These Christians lived within the Roman system; some even held jobs within the Roman legal, economic, and governmental system. But at the end of the day, their allegiance was not to Rome and Caesar; it was to Jesus. They did not put their hope in the Roman system to deliver them. Salvation, meaning, and shalom flowed only from Christ.

Liberation for the early church from the dominant myths of the Roman culture came through an acknowledgment of Christ as Lord. It is the same for us. If we are to escape hyperreality, we must acknowledge Christ as Lord. The language of Christ being in our hearts is quite helpful if we understand that it is to our hearts that temptation comes. Most people find their hearts rather than their heads lured by the false promises of hyperreality. Many of us can see at an intellectual level the tricks and traps, but it is our broken, emotional selves that become addicted by hyperreality.

So it is the human heart that ultimately needs redemption and healing. The unredeemed nature of the human heart is what causes so much suffering in our world. You will not find many people who will openly tell you that child abuse is good, that starvation and war are great, or that pollution and environmental damage are wonderful. Contrary to popular belief, very rarely can we call one group of people evil and another good. Most leaders, be they in government, business, or the military, actually are trying to do good in the best way they can, but the brokenness of the human heart subverts plans for good and replaces them with self-interest.

Our plans for good often are run aground by our dysfunctions, and this is why as a culture we are now caught in a trap. For instance, an issue such as third-world poverty or global warming is raised. People want to do something, so they get some celebrities together and put on a massive globally televised concert to raise money and awareness, but a few years later, nothing seems to have changed. I do not mean to sound cynical, for these events can be fantastic tools, but they will get us only so far if there is no transformation of human hearts. Dallas Willard, in his wonderful book *Renovation of the Heart*, wrote,

"The greatest need you and I have, the greatest need of humanity in general, is renovation of our heart. That spiritual place within us from which outlook, choices and actions come has been formed by a world denying God. It must be transformed. Indeed, the only hope for humanity lies in the fact that, just as our spirit has been formed so also can it be transformed."[10]

By acknowledging Jesus as the *true* Lord of our hearts, we enter into not just an intellectual acceptance of the beliefs of Christianity but also an intimate, living relationship that recognizes that my brokenness can be healed only by Christ and that the deepest desires of my heart can be met only by him. There is a similarity between Jesus' lordship of our hearts and the Old Testament practice of circumcision. God was telling his people that he wanted to be Lord of their lives and culture, and the sign that he chose to remind them of this relationship was right there in their pants. They could worship, pray, and read Scripture all they wanted, but when temptation came and they felt like breaking the covenant by bedding the local Babylonian hottie, they could not do so without being reminded of God's lordship. If we are to live well in God's reality, we must live under the *total* lordship of Jesus Christ.

When living under Jesus' lordship, we also recognize that he is our guide for life and that the surest way of accessing God's reality in our lives is to imitate his life. But before we can imitate his life, we must know his life, so we must therefore soak in the reality of his life as we find it in the Gospels. Often Christians believe in Jesus but do not believe in his way. His life, however, is the blueprint for true humanity. The wonderful thing is that he does not just show us the way, but he also comes with us. The Scottish theologian William Barclay explained how Christ walks with us in this way:

> Suppose we are in a strange town and we ask for directions. Suppose the person says: "Take the first to the right, and the second to the left. Cross the square, and go past the church, and take the third on the right and the road you want is the fourth road on the left." If that happens, the chances are we will get lost before we get halfway. But suppose the person we ask says: "Come. I'll take you there." In that case that person is to us the way, and we cannot miss it. That is what Jesus does for us. He not only gives us advice, he takes us by the hand and leads us. He walks beside us, strengthens, and guides us every day. He does not tell us the way: he is the way.[11]

We find peace through imitating Jesus' ministry of shalom; we find meaning through embodying Jesus' embodiment of God's reality; we find liberation from our slavery of self through Jesus' path of sacrifice; we find new life through Jesus' resurrection; we find a new home in the new world that he is building for us. If we truly are to live, we must recenter our entire lives around him who brings life. But this is not a task we can do alone.

5. HOOK INTO COUNTERCULTURAL CHRISTIAN COMMUNITY

Christianity is a community event. You cannot escape hyper-reality and live well in God's reality alone. Attempting to do so is like trying to fight fire with gasoline. The hyperreal culture thrives on individualism; to escape alone only ensures that you will return alone. Jesus, therefore, calls us to resist the powers of our day by creating a new community based on God's reality. He is not calling us to leave hyperreal culture; instead, we are to live a new way as a community *in the midst of* hyperreal culture. Doing so is the most effective way to communicate to others the "new thing" God is doing in our world. We must begin counter-cultural Christian communities that embody in the present what God is going to do in the future. You could do this through your church, your friends, your small group, or your family.

I have attempted to form community relationships through a network of communities called the Red Network, based in Melbourne.[12] We wanted to create places where young adults who have given up on Christian culture and church could come together to live out God's reality in this world. We created four communities based around urban hubs in Melbourne. The community I oversee is the East community, based in Box Hill. Box Hill Central is Melbourne's second-largest transport hub and is an incredibly multicultural area, primarily made up of Chinese but also of Vietnamese, Indian, Korean, Sudanese, Persian, Greek, Italian, and British migrants. An amazing variety of languages can be heard as one moves around the markets and shops.

We started with a group of young adults who decided to live in the area. We began not by launching a souped-up attractive service or building a worship center, but by asking, "What will it look like when God's reality comes in fullness to Box Hill? What will our neighborhood look like?" First, we spent time walking around our community, praying, observing, and imagining our community redeemed. We knew that when God's kingdom came in fullness, those who were marginalized would be honored, so we decided to reflect this honoring by aiding and befriending people who had moved into our area who were escaping from conflict in Africa. We formed a youth group of African teenagers, playing soccer, being friends, and helping with homework. I remember feeling proud as a young couple from my community told me how they were approached by a drug user suffering from heroin addiction who was trying to sell them illegal stolen goods. Their response to God's reality was to tell him that they could not buy his goods, but they decided to sit and eat with him, honoring him as an image-bearer of God. God's future will be a time in which we connect to each other in perfect love, so we encouraged people to fight against the individualism and isolation of the hyperreal world. They then began to move closer to each other. In fact, some people in the community began sharing houses, and some began to share their shopping.

We also realized that in the future God is going to usher in a time of justice that will break down the structures that keep people in poverty and oppression. We realized that God is going to remake the whole world, so we began as a community to support international campaigns for justice. One of my favorite memories is having the privilege of giving a large amount of money to a young migrant after she had had a large sum ripped off. The shock and surprise in her and her friends' faces was palpable. Her friend asked us why we would do such a thing, and I was able to tell her that we are Christians and that we are called to help.

We realized that it was our task as a community to embody celebration, so we began throwing parties and inviting people we knew just as Jesus threw a party to celebrate Matthew's decision to follow him. We realized that God was active in our community, so when we started a worship service, we began to meet in homes, a local café, and a community space. Things are nowhere near perfect in our community—we have plenty of challenges—and they will never be perfect until Christ returns to usher in God's reality in fullness. I can say with authority, however, that being part of a community that seeks to embody God's reality in our neighborhood not only aids my escape from hyperreality but incredibly enriches my life.

6. LEARN TO LIVE REDEMPTIVELY

One of the keys to living well in God's reality is learning to live redemptively. If God's reality is breaking out into this world, and if all goodness flows from the Creator, it is our duty to worship God through enjoying the goodness of his creation. This is not as easy as you may think. For it is actually notoriously difficult to enjoy life without getting caught in a number of tensions. To live well in God's reality, we must be living in God's reality. Our enjoyment of life and the good things that creation gives us must be rooted in an acknowledgment and appreciation that all goodness flows from the Creator. To live a life of enjoyment is to live a life of gratitude, to live life as a prayer of thanks.

We have already learned that our enjoyment of any activity is affected to the extent that we compare that activity with what others are doing. A man who receives a million dollars will be happy; a man who receives a million dollars while all of his friends receive a billion dollars will be sad, angry, and frustrated. By gratefully acknowledging that the goodness we receive comes from God, we don't end up ruining our enjoyment by comparing and contrasting. And by practicing this attitude of gratitude, we bring God's reality into all spheres of life. We begin the task of partnering with God in the redemption of everyday life.

One of the ways that we defeat the hold that the hyperreal culture has on us is by redeeming the ordinary. The hyperreal world tells us that we can feel pleasure only when we are doing amazing things and are leaving the ordinary world. Sadly, this is true also of much of contemporary spirituality. Spiritual writer Macrina Wiederkehr observed:

> I am concerned about the many people today who are lured to extraordinary spiritual phenomena that are manifested, it seems to me, in sensational ways. . . . The fast pace of our lives makes it difficult for us to find grace in the present moment, and when the simple gifts at our fingertips cease to nourish us, we have a tendency to crave the sensational . . . As we pine for . . . the otherworldly, there is a danger of missing a precious aspect of Christianity. We are an incarnational people. The Word was made flesh in our midst. We are rooted in an earth that God has proclaimed good.[13]

With the right attitude of worship and gratitude, we can find pleasure in even the most mundane tasks. The most ordinary things and activities directed back toward the Creator can become symphonies of joy. I discovered this a few years ago when I became very sick after contracting a virus. For seven months I stayed at home, mostly in bed. I was too sick to work, read, watch movies, or go anywhere. I had lost weight and was in constant pain. My life was miserable. I had gone from having a busy, exciting, rewarding life to being bedridden. Slowly my spirit became more and more disheartened. As I could not do much at all, I began to miss simple things that I had taken for granted—going out for dinner with my wife, catching up with friends, playing soccer with my team. For more than ten years I had been involved in full-time ministry, and just before I became ill, I had been flying to different cities, speaking to young adults about faith. My ministry was on the rise. I was used to helping, contributing, and making a difference. Now I was sick in bed, and the doctors didn't know how long I would be ill—they told me it could be years. I felt worthless.

There seemed no way in which I could gain any happiness or comfort. But then God began to speak to me. He quietly began to rebuild my spirit through the most ordinary things. One day as I lay in bed dispirited and bored, the door of my bedroom was open. And as I lay there, I began to hear sounds I never noticed before—people talking in the distance, a radio playing a tune I didn't recognize, birds singing, trees moving. I began to listen to each noise, separating them in my head, focusing on them, meditating on them. I began to realize that there was a whole world out there, alive and pulsating with the glory of God. This was God's good creation. Each insect, animal, plant, and person was lovingly formed and created by him. Creation was his love letter to me. Instead of having to be entertained and excited, I was learning to find God in the ordinary things.

Each day I would sit on my back porch, a glass of freshly squeezed orange juice in my hand and the warmth of the sun on my face, and I would simply listen to the sounds around me. This was an activity that only months earlier would have had me tapping my foot in boredom and searching out my MP3 player in order to pass the time. I began to feel a sense of God's peace that I remembered from my childhood, that sense of awe I felt as a boy as I stood in my backyard at twilight looking up at the moon. Over the years, this instinctive way of connecting with God had been dulled in me by the flashing lights of pop culture. I realized that hyperreality had cut off our ability to enjoy the pleasure that can be found in the ordinary. Nothing in the hyperreal world can compete with the treasures that can be found in the ordinary. I know that for someone caught in the constant sensory addiction that is created by our fast-paced culture, the idea of sitting on the back porch finding pleasure in drinking orange juice can hardly compete with the sexy, shiny, spectacular world of hyperreality. That is because to truly access God's reality in the ordinary, we need discipline to reorient the way in which we approach life. It is not something that can be done straightaway; we must first understand that we live in the tension of an in-between age.

God's reality is breaking out in the world, and his shalom vision is entering it; therefore deep happiness, pleasure, joy, and fulfillment can be experienced in our present-day lives. But we must understand that Christ has not yet come; the dream is not fully completed. Christians over the years have struggled to live in the tension that comes from the incompleteness of God's dream. Yes, Jesus has won the final victory over death, sin, pain, and brokenness, but the final redemption of creation is not yet here. We, therefore, are not immune from the darkness that comes from living in this in-between time when death, evil, and disease have been defeated but still have stings in their tails.

One of the problems with the way some communicate the gospel is that they interpret God's reality through the lens of consumerism; the shalom vision of the gospel becomes a self-serving, individualistic consumer lifestyle package, complete with insurance against anything bad happening to us. British church leader Steve Chalke explains:

> Shalom is the equipping of a person so they can cope with life's suffering and sorrows while basking in the beauty and joy it brings. Shalom is about comprehensive well-being and flourishing at every level of life—socially, economically, spiritually, and politically. The tragedy of what many modern-day health-and-wealth preachers have done is to take this panoramic vision of shalom and reduce it to something that merely imitates our consumerist, get-rich-quick, individualist, self-centered society.[14]

Chalke is right to point out the important fact that while God's reality breaks into our world, we are not immune from bad things happening, but that in the midst of bad things happening, we can find meaning, joy, and fulfillment through embracing a shalom vision. That is the key. Until Christ comes, we will always live in the tension between the lures of the idolatry of hyperreality and the pain and starkness of reality. But the good news for us is that not only do we have a future in God's reality, which is going to come into our world in fullness, but we can access that reality now. Pleasure, meaning, happiness, and joy can be found by following in the footsteps of Christ.

GOD'S REALITY BREAKS IN

My obsession in life aside from my family, friends, and faith is soccer. As a young boy I caught the bug, and my teen years were spent practicing, watching games on TV, and scouring magazines and newspapers for any soccer-related news. Soccer is the most popular sport in the world and the passion of hundreds of millions. But in Australia, the game holds a similar position as it does in the United States. Despite massive participation and interest, it struggles to break the media stranglehold of the local sports. Therefore, in Australia, soccer has traditionally been an underground passion, uniting all kinds of disparate racial and ethnic groups. I cherish my teen memories of playing at the local park from the end of the school day until after dark with kids of all colors, religions, and backgrounds.

I have followed the national Australian soccer team for as long as I can remember. Such a pursuit has been a painful one, as the sport has always been just on the verge of capturing the national psyche only for the team to lose in crucial games in heroic yet tragic circumstances. The unfortunate history of the sport in this country had brought a steely fanaticism to those who love the game. However, things changed after Australia defeated heavyweight Uruguay in a nail-biter to qualify for the first time in my lifetime for World Cup finals, the biggest media event on earth. There we were among the elite at Germany 2006. All of a sudden the country had caught the bug, the domestic sports were off the back page, and millions of Aussies tuned in during the dead of night to watch the Australians' first foray against the Asian champions, Japan.

We decided to watch the game at one of our church's community houses and told everyone to invite friends. We expected maybe fifteen people, but by kickoff time, easily double that number had turned out, and space was at a premium as people continued to pour into the room. I looked around the room to see friends, acquaintances, and strangers all crowding around the TV screen. In the room was a diversity of races, ranging from people whose families had been in Aus-tralia for five generations to Sudanese refugees who had been here for a year. Yet everyone was rooting for their country, Australia. Australians, because the country was started as a place to get rid of the lower classes of British society, sometimes are not as upfront about their patriotism as other countries. So I was shocked when the pictures from Germany were beamed across and I saw the stadium filled with Aussies who had traveled to the game. The joke is that Australians don't know the words to our national anthem, but the hairs on the back of my neck stood up as the Australian national anthem was played and the crowd belted it out with deafening results. I had been waiting for this moment all my soccer-loving life.

The game began with the Aussies playing well, but everyone in the room felt nervous as we wondered if our bad luck would strike again as it so often had on a big occasion. And then it did. The Japanese scored a goal that millions around the world—except for the referee—judged as a foul. We were shattered; the hope in the room seemed to fade, and fun gave way to frustration. The Aussies kept pressing forward, trying to score. With world champion Brazil coming up in the next game, being defeated by Japan would mean disaster. Nothing was going right; our shots just missed.

Because of the low level of scoring in soccer, single mistakes can ruin games, so watching this game was an excruciating experience. *How could things have gone so badly?* I thought. Everything was primed, yet we were about to go out on an illegal goal. Then, with seconds to go, the miraculous happened. Substitute Tim Cahill, out of nowhere, smashed home the equalizing goal.

Now, Australians, particularly Aussie men, are pretty reserved and quiet. Other cultures are good at showing emotions, as in America, where celebrating with whoops and high fives is common. But when an Australian really celebrates, months, if not years, of repressed emotions and feelings come exploding out in an almost guttural, primal *yyyeeeEESSSSS!!!*

As the goal was scored, the room detonated. Bodies flew into the air and inhibitions flew out the door. The roar lasted for at least a minute, and two days later my ears were still ringing. The scene was more akin to a death metal mosh pit than a lounge room. As I jumped up and down, I noticed that we had smashed all of the plates and cups that we had been drinking from. And days later we noticed that almost superhumanly there were handprints on the high ceiling.

Before we had sat down, Australia had scored again. We were now winning. This was unimaginable! We then scored again, and the celebrations continued. I could hear cars honking in the street and other households cheering in the dead of night. As everyone else continued jumping around like disinhibited four-year-olds, I sank into my chair, physically spent, with a giant smile on my face and virtually no voice left, and surveyed the wondrous scene. People were hugging and high-fiving people they did not know. Through the mash of celebrating bodies, I could see my friend, Auyen, a refugee from Sudan, dancing in that joyous way that only Africans can, head down, moving his body in total celebration. Satisfaction pulsed through my body. Then it dawned on me: *This is what it will be like when God's reality breaks into our world in fullness. This is how this chapter of humanity's history ends.* I wanted to cry. God was speaking to me, telling me that this panorama of unadulterated and complete joy is a glimpse of what is in our future.

One day you will wake up, and everything will seem brighter, infinitely better, and the air will be fresher. You will look out your window, and the world will be remade. You will run into the street to find that death, disease, suffering, injustice, and pain are gone, and you will embrace friends and strangers, barely able to contain your delight. Then you will realize that God is walking among us, that he is totally reconnected to his people. This is our future.

But if you listen now, really open your ears, listen past the pop songs, the Hollywood soundtracks, and the advertising jingles of the hyperreal world, you can hear the roar of celebration. It is faint, but it is getting stronger. It is coming up from the tenements, bouncing off the walls of projects and favelas, roaring out from African villages, reverberating around lonely suburban streets. Can you hear it? It's the sound of God's reality knocking on the walls of your reality. It's the sound of everything your soul truly wishes for coming true. Will you join the party?

Notes

Chapter 1: Why Your Faith Does Not Work

1. Krishan Kumar, "Hyper-Reality," in *The New Fontana Dictionary of Modern Thought*, Alan Bullock, Stephen Trombley, eds. (London: HarperCollins, 1999), 409.

Chapter 2: Welcome to Hyperreality

1. Vincent Miller, *Consuming Religion: Christian Faith and Practice in a Consumer Culture* (New York: Continuum, 2003), 59–60.

Chapter 3: The Whole of Life As Shopping: Hyperconsumerism

1. Daniel Harris, *Cute, Quaint, Hungry and Romantic: The Aesthetics of Consumerism* (New York: Basic Books, 2000), 75–76.
2. John F. Kavanaugh, *Following Christ in a Consumer Society: The Spirituality of Cultural Resistance* (Maryknoll, NY: Orbis, 1991), 31.
3. Christopher Lasch, *The Culture of Narcissism* (Suffolk, UK: Abacus, 1979), 7.
4. Jeremy Rifkin, *The Age of Access: The New Culture of Hypercapitalism Where All of Life Is a Paid-For Experience* (New York: Penguin Putnam, 2000), 7.

Chapter 4: Hyperconsumerism As Religion

1. Kevin Roberts, *Lovemarks: The Future Beyond Brands* (Millers Point, NSW, Australia: Murdoch, 2004), 58.
2. Helen Trinca and Catherine Fox, *Better Than Sex: How a Whole Generation Got Hooked on Work* (Milson's Point, NSW, Australia: Random House, 2004), 61.
3. Peter Brierley, "Implicit Religion," in C. Partridge and D. Groothuis, eds., *Dictionary of Contemporary Religion in the Western World* (Leicester: InterVarsity, 2002), 243.
4. Lesslie Newbigin, *The Open Secret: An Introduction to the Theology of Mission* (Grand Rapids: Eerdmans, 1985), 160–61.
5. Dallas Willard, *The Divine Conspiracy: Rediscovering Our Hidden Life in God* (San Francisco: HarperCollins, 1998), 341.
6. Kavanaugh, *Following Christ in a Consumer Society*, 5.

Chapter 5: It's All About You!

1. Duane Elmer, *Cross-Cultural Conflict: Building Effective Relationships for Ministry* (Downers Grove, IL: InterVarsity, 1993), 25.
2. Zygmunt Bauman, *Liquid Love: On the Frailty of Human Bonds* (Cambridge, UK: Polity, 2003), 58.

Chapter 6: How Hyperreality Makes Us Unhappy

1. Ruth Tucker, *From Jerusalem to Irian Jaya: A Biographical History of Christian Missions* (Grand Rapids: Zondervan, 1983), 47.
2. *Daily Free Press* (Boston University), November 16, 2000, http://www. radicalmiddle.com/x_psych_deprn.htm.
3. David Myers, *The American Paradox: Spiritual Hunger in an Age of Plenty* (New Haven, CT: Yale University Press, 2000), 138.
4. Richard Layard, *Happiness: Lessons from a New Science* (London: Penguin, 2005), 33.
5. Ibid.
6. Alain de Botton, *Status Anxiety* (London: Penguin, 2004).
7. Layard, *Happiness*, 45.
8. Barney Schwartz, *The Paradox of Choice: Why More Is Less* (New York: HarperCollins, 2004), 2.
9. Ibid., 20.
10. K. Lasn and B. Grierson, "Malignant Sadness," *Adbusters*, June–July 2000, PAGE.
11. Jean Twenge, *Generation Me: Why Today's Young Americans Are More Confident, Assertive, Entitled—and More Miserable Than Ever Before* (New York: Free Press, 2006), 83.
12. Ibid., 84.
13. Thanks to my friend Nick Wight for this insight.
14. A. Robbins and A. Wilner, *Quarterlife Crisis: The Unique Challenge of Life in Your Twenties* (New York: Tarcher Putnam, 2001), 4.

Chapter 7: The Rub Between Real Life and Hyperreality

1. Ash Barker, *Surrender All: A Call to Sub-Merge with Christ* (Springvale, VIC, Australia: Urban Neighbours of Hope, 2005), 5–6.
2. Henri Nouwen, *Reaching Out: The Three Movements of the Spiritual Life* (New York: Image Books, 1975), 26–27.
3. Kavanaugh, *Following Christ in a Consumer Society*, 6.
4. Gordon Wenham, *Life and Death and the Consumerist Ethic* in C. Bartholomew and T. Moritz, eds., *Christ and Consumerism: A Critical Analysis of the Spirit of the Age* (Carlisle: Paternoster, 2000), 127.

5.   Jürgen Moltmann, *The Source: The Holy Spirit and the Theology of Life* (London: SCM, 1997), 107.

Chapter 8: How Hyperreality Ruins Faith
1.   M. Buber, *Tales of the Hasidim* (New York: Schocken, 1975), 243–44.
2.   Walter Brueggemann, "Genesis," in *Bible Commentary for Teaching and Preaching* (Atlanta: John Knox, 1982), 53–54.
3.   Nikolai Berdyaev, *Slavery and Freedom* (New York: Scribner, 1944), 59.
4.   Abraham Heschel, *A Philosophy of Judaism* (New York: Farrar, Straus and Giroux, 1955), 119.
5.   Alan Hirsch, *The Forgotten Ways: Reactivating the Missional Church* (Grand Rapids: Brazos, 2006), 88.
6.   Eugene Peterson, *Christ Plays in Ten Thousand Places: A Conversation in Spiritual Theology* (London: Hodder and Stoughton, 2005), 254.
7.   Kavanaugh, *Following Christ in a Consumer Society*, 58.

Chapter 9: Hyperreal Christianity
1.   N. T. Wright, *The Challenge of Jesus: Rediscovering Who Jesus Was and Is* (Downers Grove, IL: InterVarsity, 1999), 96.
2.   Ibid., 9.
3.   Bernard Salt, *The Big Picture: Life, Work and Relationship in the 21st Century* (Melbourne: Hardie Grant, 2006), 73.
4.   Paul Hiebert, *Anthropological Insights for Missionaries* (Grand Rapids: Baker, 1985), 222.
5.   Ibid.
6.   Ibid., 223.
7.   J. Rowbotham, "Life's On-Call Butler: How Teens View God," *The Australian*, March 4, 2006.

Chapter 10: Good-bye to the Plastic Jesus of Hyperreality
1.   Brad Young, *Jesus: The Jewish Theologian* (Peabody, MA: Hendrickson, 1995), 58.
2.   Ravi Zacharias, *Jesus Among the Other Gods: The Absolute Claims of the Christian Message* (Nashville: Nelson, 2000), 87.
3.   Dallas Willard, *The Divine Conspiracy: Rediscovering Our Hidden Life in God* (San Francisco: HarperCollins, 1998), 3.
4.   Allen Wakabayashi, *Kingdom Come: How Jesus Wants to Change the World* (Downers Grove, IL: InterVarsity, 2003), 38–39.
5.   L. Ryken, J. Wilhoit, and T. Longman, eds., *Dictionary of Biblical Imagery* (Downers Grove, IL: InterVarsity, 1998), 117.

6. Kushner, *When All You've Ever Wanted Isn't Enough*, 82.
7. John Piper, *Desiring God: Meditations of a Christian Hedonist* (Portland, OR: Multnomah, 1986), 19.
8. Kushner, *When All You've Ever Wanted Isn't Enough*, 82.

Chapter 11: A Fight for the Future
1. Randy Alcorn, *Heaven* (Wheaton: Tyndale, 2004), 17.
2. For a detailed explanation, see R. Tarnas, "The Greek World View," in R. Tarnas, ed., *The Passion of the Western Mind: Understanding the Ideas That Have Shaped Our World View* (London: Plimlico, 1991).
3. Millard Erickson, *Christian Theology* (Grand Rapids: Baker, 1983), 1235.
4. Wayne Grudem, *Bible Doctrine: Essential Teachings of the Christian Faith* (Leicester: InterVarsity, 1999), 465.
5. N. T. Wright, *Following Jesus: Biblical Reflections on Discipleship* (London: SPCK, 1994), 85.
6. Alcorn, *Heaven*, 45.
7. Heschel, *A Philosophy of Judaism*, 46.
8. C. S. Lewis, quoted in W. Vaus, *Mere Theology: A Guide to the Thought of C. S. Lewis* (Downers Grove, IL: InterVarsity, 2004), 215.
9. Chaim Potok in M. Buber, *Tales of the Hasidim* (New York: Schocken, 1975), xi.
10. Alcorn, *Heaven*, 17.

Chapter 12: God's Reality Now
1. Kushner, *When All You've Ever Wanted Isn't Enough*, 23.
2. C. S. Lewis, *The Great Divorce* (New York: HarperCollins, 1946), 117–20.
3. Tim Kasser, *The High Price of Materialism* (Cambridge, MA: MIT Press, 2002), 47–48.
4. Ronald Sider, *The Scandal of the Evangelical Conscience: Why Are Christians Living Just Like the Rest of the World?* (Grand Rapids: Baker, 2005), 17.
5. E. Stanley Jones, *Abundant Living* (London: Hodder & Stoughton, 1946), 11.
6. Teresa of Avila, *Interior Castle* (New York: Doubleday, 1961), 7.

Chapter 13: Six Keys to Living Well Within God's Reality
1. Companion curriculum to this book, including *The Trouble with Paris DVD Study*, is available from Thomas Nelson, Inc.
2. R. Layard, *Happiness: Lessons from a New Science* (London: Penguin, 2005), 66.

3. Ibid.
4. Barry Schwartz, *The Paradox of Choice: Why More Is Less* (New York: HarperCollins, 2004), 107.
5. Robert Putnam, *Bowling Alone: The Collapse and Revival of American Community* (New York: Simon & Schuster, 2000).
6. Layard, *Happiness: Lessons from a New Science*, 72.
7. R. A. Emmons et al., *Assessing Spirituality Through Personal Goals: Implications for Research on Religion and Subjective Well-Being.* (Article in *Social Indicators Research Journal:* Springer. Netherlands. Volume 45, November 1998), 404, quoted in C. Hamilton, *Growth Fetish* (Crows Nest, NSW, Australia: Allen & Unwin, 2003), 51.
8. Michael Green, *Evangelism in the Early Church* (East Sussex, UK: Highland Books, 1970), 137.
9. Newbigin, *The Open Secret*, 3.
10. Dallas Willard, *Renovation of the Heart: Putting on the Character of Christ* (Leicester: InterVarsity, 2002), 3.
11. William Barclay, quoted in D. Andrews, *Christi-Anarchy: Discovering a Radical Spirituality of Compassion* (Oxford: Lion, 1999), 115.
12. For more on the story of the Red Network, see A. Hirsch, *The Forgotten Ways: Reactivating the Missional Church* (Grand Rapids: Brazos, 2006), or visit www.red.org.au.
13. Macrina Wiederkehr, *A Tree Full of Angels: Seeing God in the Ordinary* (San Francisco: HarperCollins: 1995).
14. Steve Chalke and A. Mann, *The Lost Message of Jesus* (Grand Rapids: Zondervan, 2003), 37.